GOLF
IS A
FUNNY
GAME

Other Books by Allan Zullo

G O L F
IS A
FUNNY
GAME

by Allan Zullo
with Chris Rodell

**Andrews McMeel
Publishing, LLC**

Kansas City

08 09 10 11 12 WKT 10 9 8 7 6 5 4 3 2 1
ISBN-13: 978-0-7407-7122-4
ISBN-10: 0-7407-7122-1

Library of Congress Control Number: 2007934893

ATTENTION: SCHOOLS AND BUSINESSES

Andrews McMeel books are available at quantity discounts with bulk purchase for educational, business, or sales promotional use. For information, please write to: Special Sales Department, Andrews McMeel Publishing, LLC, 4520 Main Street, Kansas City, Missouri 64111.

To the Linquist boys, Frank for the skill he brings to his game and Ike for the laughter he brings to his game.

—AZ

CONTENTS

TEEING OFF

More than any other sport, golf generates the most outbursts of rage and passion—and belly laughs.

This centuries-old sport boasts a rich heritage of zany moments from tee to green. It's not just the ignoble incident or outrageous shot that provokes laughter. Often, it's what the golfer or playing partner says right afterwards that's truly hilarious.

Yes, we bemoan the bunkers and bogeys, the chili dips and recurring yips. We curse our shanks and slices, our buried lies and plugged lies. But by the 19th hole, all the doubles and triples we made are forgotten. And then begins one of the great traditions of the game: regaling fellow linksmen with good-natured putdowns and comebacks as we relive all those banana balls, topped balls, and lost balls. We might not find it so humorous at the time when we duck-hook a drive, bunker-whiff a sand wedge, or deep-six an approach. But looking back, those confounding moments provide the seed (some might say fertilizer) for hilarious stories that will be retold for years to come.

This book is a collection of more than 200 entertaining true anecdotes, almost all of them capped by a classic quip executed by the golfer with the precision of a flawless bunker shot into the cup. The stories range from the days of hickory shafts to the 2007 season and involve current members of the PGA, Champions, and LPGA tours as well as past professionals and amateurs of all ages and skills. (A few stories include expletives that might seem offensive to some people, but these are words that have been shouted and heard on every tee, fairway, and green of every course in the world.)

Whether it's the hacker who caught his own ricocheted drive, the pro who stripped down to his shorts to play a shot, or the caddie who lost a golf bag during a round, one thing is certain: Golf is a funny game.

GOLF
IS A
FUNNY
GAME

FRIEND or FOE

PUTT NUT

South African Simon Hobday, who won the 1994 U.S. Senior Open, and fellow countryman and pro Dale Hayes challenged Rhodesians Mark McNulty and Nick Price in a series of exhibitions in Europe in the early 1980s.

For years, McNulty, known on the European Tour for his putting prowess, had used the same putter, a Bullseye with a blue grip. The manufacturer stopped making that model in the late 1970s.

However, Hobday was in a pro shop one day when he spotted an old, used Bullseye that was the same model and had the same blue grip as McNulty's, so he bought it. Before the next exhibition,

Hobday secretly replaced the cherished putter in McNulty's bag with the old one while McNulty wasn't looking.

Hundreds of spectators had gathered around the 1st tee while Hayes, acting as the emcee, introduced McNulty. "Most of you know Mark for his incredible putting prowess."

Interrupting Hayes, Hobday shouted, "Where is that bloody putter?" He stomped over to McNulty's bag, whipped out the Bullseye, and broke it over his knee.

His eyes wide in disbelief and horror, McNulty gasped and stood in stunned silence at what Hobday had done to his all-time favorite putter. McNulty's shock slowly turned to rage. Just as McNulty was about to go after Hobday, the jokester's caddie produced McNulty's prized Bullseye and saved McNulty from a heart attack or attempted murder charges.

NO MISTAKEN IDENTITY

Tom Weiskopf was stretching moments before he was to pair up with Jack Nicklaus in the final round of the 1978 Masters. Both players were six strokes behind, not totally out of contention but not really threatening. After

Weiskopf finished warming up, he spotted Nicklaus coming off the range and muttered, "I don't believe it." He and the Bear were dressed in exactly the same color shirt and same color pants.

Weiskopf turned to his wife, Jeanne, and said, "Please go to the pro shop and buy me a different color shirt. It's just too weird to be dressed exactly like the guy you're playing with."

While Jeanne hustled off, a tournament official came over to Weiskopf and whispered, "Tom, I don't want to upset you, but it's my responsibility to tell you that Jack has received a death threat today. We have to consider it as being serious. There will be some FBI guys and some security in the gallery. And I'm going to be with you, very close but outside the ropes. I just wanted you to know."

Weiskopf arrived at the 1st tee and grinned when he saw that Nicklaus had just realized they were wearing the same color clothes. Then Jeanne showed up with the new shirt. Weiskopf took off his shirt right there on the 1st tee, prompting the gallery to whistle and shout.

Nicklaus strolled over to Weiskopf and said, "Tom, what in the hell are you doing?"

"Changing shirts," said Weiskopf. Then with a wink he added, "I just want to make sure they don't shoot the wrong guy."

LOST CAUSE

Tom Watson was paired with NBA all-star Charles Barkley at a pro-am event in 2000. Barkley was as bad a golfer as he was a great basketball player.

During the round, Watson tried everything he could think of to help Barkley, offering him tips on his grip, swing, and stance. But nothing worked. By the 4th hole, Watson sighed and told Barkley, "I'm sorry, Charles. I've run out of ideas. I feel for you. I really do."

IT MAID SENSE

LPGA stars Grace Park and Cristie Kerr, who are close friends, were locked in a final-round duel at the 2003 Michelob Light Open on the River Course at Kingsmill near Williamsburg, Virginia. Park ended the suspense by sinking a dramatic twenty-foot putt on the 18th green to beat Kerr by a single stroke.

After leaving the scorer's tent, Kerr was asked by a reporter whether she was upset by Park's winning putt. Kerr replied, "She's one of the bridesmaids in my wedding. I can't be mad at her."

GUARDIAN SPIRIT

In 1993, President Bill Clinton played the Mauna Kea Golf Course in Hawaii with John Waihee III, the state's governor.

At one particular tee on the seaside course, Waihee told the president, "Hit the ball a little right of the center of the fairway." Clinton drove his ball a long way, but it drifted too far to the right and disappeared over a slight rise.

"Oh, oh," clucked the governor. "Looks like you're in the lava bed."

"Why didn't you tell me there was lava over there?" asked Clinton.

Replied the governor, "You didn't ask."

As Waihee prepared to tee off, he mentioned that he was a direct descendant of King Kamehameha, who unified the Hawaiian Islands. "We really believe in ancestor guardians so we can continue the spirit," said the governor.

Then he drove his ball almost exactly to the spot where Clinton had lost his. But when Waihee's ball hit the lava bed, it bounced back out onto the middle of the fairway. The governor grinned and said, "See? I told you."

Replied Clinton, "Where do I convert?"

COLORED VIEWPOINT

Tommy Armour, one of the top pros in the 1920s and 1930s, was a keen observer of people.

One time he teamed up in a pro-am with a golfer who played the first round in an all-blue outfit that matched his blue headcovers and shoes. The amateur shot a 95.

The next day, the duffer came out in an all-red outfit with matching red bag, shirt, and shoes. This time he shot a 96.

After the second round, he told Armour, "I would really appreciate any comments you have about my golf game."

Armour thought for several seconds and then said, "I think you're a shot better in blue."

LOST AND FOUND

Avid golfers Carroll Stonehouse and Ray Sivers were playing golf at the Highlands Country Club in Grand Rapids, Michigan, in 1997 when Sivers hit a nasty shot into the thick woods bordering the 15th hole.

Figuring the ball might have hit a tree and bounced back into the open, they drove their cart up a hill. They couldn't see the ball. After a few minutes, Stonehouse said, "No way do we go in those woods and look for your ball. There're poison ivy and prickers galore in there."

"Don't worry, I'll find it," said Sivers.

Just then they heard a little beeping sound. "The ball is making that sound," said Sivers. Sure enough, he found his beeping ball. "That's the best ball made," he told his playing partner. "You can never lose it."

"Geez, that's pretty neat," said Stonehouse. "Where'd you get it?"

Replied Sivers, "I found it in the woods one day."

WHAT'S THE MEANING OF THIS?

Insurance executive Stanley Cohen and his playing partner Dr. Roger Freilich, both of West Palm Beach, Florida, went golfing one day in 1995 at the Palm Beach Gardens Municipal Course. They were hooked up with two retired and distinguished Canadian men who were on vacation.

The foursome teed off and began a pleasant round. Cohen and Freilich understood they were in the company of two refined men—one a former judge—who were quite mannerly. The Americans made a point of watching their own language after bad shots—of which there were several—because they didn't want to offend their playing partners.

Cohen and Freilich couldn't help but notice that every time the judge sent a ball out of bounds or onto the wrong fairway, he would mutter "AMF." Because he was shanking and slicing his shots throughout the round, they heard him say "AMF" many times.

Cohen's curiosity over its meaning was growing by the hole. Finally at the 15th tee, he felt compelled to ask after the judge once again uttered "AMF" after another wayward drive. "Pardon me, Judge," said Cohen, "but just what does 'AMF' mean?"

The prim and proper jurist turned to Cohen and replied simply, "Adios, motherfucker."

BOTTLE FATIGUE

In his rookie year in 1975, Roger Maltbie was playing in the Greater Jacksonville Open. He barely made the cut and then had a lousy third round. So to drown his sorrows, Maltbie went into the Swingers' Tent, a canvas-covered area where golfers and VIPs could party to live music and eat and drink to their hearts' content. Because he wasn't playing well in the tournament, he got hammered and was one of the last to leave.

Unfortunately, he was one of the first ones scheduled to tee off on Sunday.

His caddie, David Larson, rousted Maltbie out of bed and dragged the hung-over golfer to the practice tee. Still woozy, Maltbie hit a wedge seventy-five yards past his target. Then he topped the next one.

"This ain't gonna work," Maltbie muttered. He shuffled off the practice area and plopped down under an oak tree. "Wake me when it's my time to tee off," he told Larson. Then the golfer fell asleep for the entire warm-up period.

Larson awakened Maltbie and escorted him to the 1st hole. The bleary-eyed golfer was paired with happy-go-lucky Joe Porter and serious-minded Australian David Graham (who later won the 1979 PGA Championship and the 1981 U.S. Open).

On his opening drive, Maltbie, who was still trying to get his bearings, squibbed the ball, and it skirted into the lake. He looked at his stunned playing partners and began to laugh. "I can't believe I hit the ball," he said.

"You mean you can't believe you hit the ball in the water?" asked Graham.

"No," replied Maltbie. "I mean I really didn't think I was going to be able to hit the ball at all."

Somehow, Maltbie managed to bogey the first two holes and was on the green of the 3rd hole. It was a nippy, windy March morning, yet he was soaking wet from the cold sweats and had wrapped a towel around his neck.

As he stood over a twelve-foot putt, he raised up and said, "Excuse me." Then he ran into the woods and threw up. Because the threesome teed off early, there was no gallery to witness his upchucking. Maltbie returned to the green and promptly drained his putt. Porter burst out laughing that his sick playing partner could par the hole.

Feeling much better, Maltbie chipped and one-putted his way around the golf course and ended up shooting an even par 72.

Meanwhile, Graham, who hit the ball well but suffered some unlucky bounces and was betrayed by a balky putter, finished with a 74. As he signed his scorecard, Graham groused, "That's it. I'm quitting this bloody game when a man can come out on the course completely drunk and still beat me."

TURNING POINT

On his way to capturing the 1946 PGA Championship, Ben Hogan clobbered Jimmy Demaret by a lopsided score of 10 and 9 during the semifinals (when it was match play) at Portland (Oregon) Golf Club.

Shortly after signing his scorecard, Demaret was asked by reporters to describe the turning point of the match. Replied the vanquished golfer, "When Hogan showed up."

THE TALL AND
THE SHORT OF IT

At the 1978 Houston Open at Woodlands (Texas) Country Club, Gary Player was 6 behind going into the final round.

Andy Bean, who was on the leaderboard, went up to the five-foot, seven-inch Player and jokingly told him, "You're not going to win this week, you South African midget."

Player went out and shot a 64 to capture the tournament by one stroke over Bean, a Georgia native who had spent many of his teenage years in central Florida. After they signed their scorecards, Player playfully jabbed the towering six-foot, four-inch Bean in the ribs and cracked, "That's how I handle big rednecks like you here in Texas."

THUNDER AND LIGHTNING

There was no love lost between American Tommy "Thunder" Bolt and Scottish pro Eric Brown during the 1957 Ryder Cup at Lindrick Golf Club in England.

The Americans, who had won every cup since 1935, jumped out to a 3–1 lead in the foursomes. Even though Bolt and teammate Dick Mayer won their match, Bolt was furious with the pro-British crowd, calling them "the worst in the world."

He complained to the press, "They cheered when I missed a putt and sat on their hands when I hit a good shot. Individually they are pretty nice folks. But get them together and they are about as miserable a bunch of people as you could ever have the misfortune to run into in a supposedly civilized world."

Brown, who could be just as fiery as the American, took offense at Bolt's scathing criticism. Through the press, he told Bolt to shut up and play.

The next day, British captain Dai Rees gambled on sending out Brown, a tough match player, first in the singles, hoping he could beat the equally aggressive Bolt. Brown relished the challenge.

When the two had not appeared on the tee as the start time approached, American Jimmy Demaret cracked, "They're out on the practice ground throwing clubs at each other from fifty paces."

After falling 3 down early on, Bolt deliberately played slowly, trying to knock the lightning-quick Brown off stride. The ploy failed. To the delight of the crowd, Brown sent his caddie off to the clubhouse to fetch a chair, which he sat in while waiting for Bolt to hit.

Brown went on to win the ill-tempered match, 4 and 3, sparking a dramatic comeback as the British won six of the eight singles matches to capture the cup, 7½–4½.

After Brown dispatched Bolt, there was no shaking of hands.

"I guess you won, but I didn't enjoy it one bit," groused Bolt.

Brown retorted, "And nor would I after the licking I just gave you."

ON THE SHADY SIDE

The great Walter Hagen was about to play an exhibition match near Orlando, Florida, on a stiflingly hot afternoon. Despite the sweltering heat, a crowd had gathered at the 1st tee.

The organizer of the event apologized to the Haig for the conditions. "I'm sorry it's so hot, Mr. Hagen," said the club chairman. "It's 105 in the shade."

Hagen dabbed his forehead with his silk hankie and said, "I'm sure glad we don't have to play in the shade."

STAKE OUT

Roger Maltbie and Hale Irwin were tied after the regulation seventy-two holes in the inaugural Memorial Tournament at Muirfield Village in Dublin, Ohio, in 1976. That meant a three-hole playoff starting on the 15th hole, and if that didn't settle the matter, it would go to sudden death.

Irwin—winner up to then of seven Tour events, including the 1974 U.S. Open—was the odds-on favorite to beat the long-haired, floppy-mustachioed, plaid-

A DANGEROUS TREND

On February 2, 1949, about 150 miles east of El Paso, Texas, Ben Hogan's car collided head-on with a passing Greyhound bus. The impact drove the engine into the driver's seat and the steering wheel into the back seat. Although his wife, Valerie, sustained only minor injuries, Hogan suffered a broken collarbone, a smashed rib, a double fracture of the pelvis, and a broken ankle. While in the hospital, he developed a serious blood clot and needed emergency surgery.

Yet 16 months after the near-fatal accident, Hogan astonished the golf world by contending for the 1950 U.S. Open at Merion Golf Club near Philadelphia. After an amazing 1-iron to the green on the final hole in the final round, Hogan tied Lloyd Mangrum and George Fazio, forcing a three-way playoff.

Rifling his drives squarely down the fairway and landing his approach shots with deadly accuracy, Hogan surged to victory in the extra round.

As he shook Hogan's hand and congratulated him, Mangrum said, "Well, Ben, you've started a new trend."

"What's that, Lloyd?" asked Hogan.

"We're all going out tonight and try to get hit by a bus."

pants—wearing winner of two tournaments. They both birdied the 15th and parred the 16th.

On the 17th, Irwin drove into the fairway, but Maltbie pulled the ball left, and it sailed toward the gallery. Unexpectedly, the ball emerged from the gallery and bounced onto the green, settling about twenty-five feet from the cup.

Irwin, miffed at his opponent's good luck, glowered at Maltbie and then hit his approach about fifteen feet behind the hole.

As Maltbie walked down the fairway, he was worried his ball had hit a spectator in the head before rebounding onto the green. But then he learned that his ball had struck a gallery rope stake and received a most fortunate bounce. Maltbie took full advantage of the fluke and parred the hole. Still rattled by the break, Irwin missed his birdie putt and settled for a par, forcing sudden death.

Maltbie birdied the next hole to win the Memorial title. Minutes later, Irwin was giving an interview in the pressroom while Maltbie stood in the back waiting for his turn to speak. A marshal walked in holding the stake and whispered to the winner, "I thought you might like to have this."

Maltbie took it and held it aloft as if offering it to Irwin.

Irwin groused, "No thanks. I've already had the shaft once today."

TO COIN A PHRASE

At the 1985 Ryder Cup at the Belfry Golf & Country Club in Sutton, Coldfield, England, Lanny Wadkins and Mark O'Meara were paired up against Europe's Seve Ballesteros and Miguel Pinero in a four-ball match on the second day.

On the 1st green, Ballesteros's coin was in Wadkins's line, so the American asked him to move it. The Spaniard nudged it a few inches out of the way. Wadkins then badly pulled his putt. But in an incredibly lucky break, his ball struck the coin, glanced to the right, and rolled into the cup.

Ballesteros was furious and shouted, "You do that on purpose! You make me move my coin so you bounce the ball off of it!"

Wadkins rolled his eyes and said, "That's right, Seve. I'm that fucking good."

HOPE JEST

Comedian Bob Hope was playing with his friend, producer Sam Goldwyn, at Lakeside Country Club when Goldwyn blew an easy two-foot putt. In a rage, he hurled his putter into a bush, vowing never to use that club again.

As Goldwyn stormed on to the next tee, Hope quietly picked up the discarded putter and slipped it into his own bag.

When it was Hope's turn to putt on the next green, he used Goldwyn's putter and sank a twenty-footer. Goldwyn was impressed and asked whether he could try Hope's putter. Hope obliged. After examining the club carefully, Goldwyn tried a few practice putts and then said, "I like this putter very much. Will you sell it to me?"

"Sure," said Hope with a perfectly straight face. So Goldwyn happily—but unwittingly—bought back his own putter for $50.

WIGGLE WAGGLE

Scottish pro Sandy Herd, who won the British Open in 1902, made an incredible number of appearances in the annual tournament, spanning more than fifty years. Fittingly, he debuted in his hometown of St. Andrews in 1885 at the age of seventeen. He last appeared in the event in 1939 when he was seventy-one, also at St. Andrews.

But what Herd was most famous for was his time-consuming habit that preceded every shot. He took an untold number of waggles with his club before he struck the ball. Although his habit often irked impatient playing partners, one of his defenders reminded them, "His waggles are many but his shots are few."

One time during a tournament, as Herd addressed the ball, an annoyed playing partner began counting the waggles in a stage whisper: ". . . twelve, thirteen, fourteen."

Herd stopped, looked up at his fellow golfer, and said, "Laddie, ye cannot count. That was fifteen. Now we'll start all over again."

CALLING HIS SHOT

Moe Norman was an eccentric Canadian golfer who is considered one of the most accurate ball strikers the game has ever seen.

One time in Toronto in 1969, Moe played an exhibition match with Sam Snead and Ed "Porky" Oliver. On one particular par-4 hole, a creek crossed the fairway about 240 yards from the tee. Norman reached for his driver.

"This is a lay-up hole, Moe," Snead told him. "You can't clear the creek with a driver."

"Not trying to," Norman said. "I'm playing for the bridge."

Snead's and Oliver's tee shots ended up safely on the near side of the water. Norman then hit his drive. His playing partners watched in awe as the ball landed just short of the creek, bounced onto the bridge, rolled across it, and stopped on the other side.

BUGABOO

Comedian George Lopez and oddball pro Jesper Parnevik were paired at the 2005 AT&T Pebble Beach National Pro-Am.

At the 10th hole at Poppy Hills, Parnevik shanked a ball that never got off the ground and went forty yards into the woods.

"What happened?" asked Lopez.

"During my downswing I saw that a ladybug had landed on my ball," Parnevik explained. "I didn't want to hit it, so I tried to pull out of the shot."

"I've got a new name for you," said Lopez. "From now on you're Lovebug."

YANKEE SWINGERS

When Roger Clemens played for the New York Yankees, he considered himself baseball's greatest golf nut.

"I'll play in any weather, including sleet," he'd tell his teammates. "Anybody can play in good weather."

In 1999, after pitching seven and a third innings in a nighttime win at Yankee Stadium, Clemens got to bed at 2 A.M. But because it was an off day, he woke up at 5:30 A.M. on a rainy day to make an 8 A.M. tee time with two teammates at the Westchester Country Club outside New York City.

Playing with him were pitcher Andy Pettitte (known as Lefty on the scorecard) and designated hitter Chili Davis, aka Dawg. Sports columnist Thomas Boswell joined the trio.

Like pro golfers, the ballplayers needled each other during the game. After Pettitte hit a short but straight drive that landed in the fairway, Davis cracked, "That's a condom shot. It doesn't feel good, but it's safe."

Pettitte teased Davis about the huge head on his Ping ISI titanium driver. "I need all of it," Davis claimed. "The bigger the headache, the bigger the pill."

When Davis hit a snap hook, Clemens crowed, "At Fenway, that's a double off the tin."

On this day, Pettitte shot 89, and Clemens and Davis each carded 83. Said Davis as they strolled to the 19th hole, "Someday I gotta give up baseball. It hurts my golf swing."

DOING WHAT COMES NATURALLY

For many years, fellow comedians George Burns and Harpo Marx played golf together nearly every week. Whereas Harpo took the game seriously and shot in the low 80s, Burns didn't care much for the game but played because it gave him something to do. Often, while going toward his ball, he sang and cracked jokes.

One day Burns was playing with Harpo, who was having the best round of his life. They reached the tee of a long par-5 where a small green was surrounded by sand traps at the top of a steep incline. Sure enough, Harpo's third shot landed in one of the bunkers.

Because Burns didn't want to disturb Harpo or make him nervous, Burns stayed at the bottom of the hill while Harpo climbed to the top. When Harpo was ready to hit from the trap, he looked at Burns and said, "What are you doing down there, George?"

"You're one under par. I don't want to upset you by watching you hit out of the trap."

"You're upsetting me by staying down there. Come on up here and watch me, like you always do."

So Burns trudged up the hill and stood on the edge of the trap. As Harpo prepared to strike the ball, he noticed that Burns was looking the other way.

"Why aren't you watching me, George, like you always do?" Harpo asked.

Burns explained again, "Harpo, I don't want to upset you. You're one under par."

"You're upsetting me right now. Please, do what you always do."

Just as Harpo took his back swing, Burns broke out in song with "When Irish Eyes Are Smiling." Harpo missed the ball completely, which was the end of his under-par round.

"Why are you singing?" Harpo demanded.

Burns replied, "Harpo, you asked me to do what I always do. So I did."

NAME CHANGE

Before a pro-am event, PGA Tour player Jerry Kelly innocently asked an amateur on the putting green, "Which pro did your group draw to play with?"

The amateur grunted and said, "We had a chance of getting Tiger, but we ended up getting Jerry fucking Kelly."

Kelly smiled, extended his hand out and said, "Hi, I'm Jerry fucking Kelly."

CHAIN OF FOOLS

Actor Jack Lemmon made twenty-five celebrated appearances at the AT&T Pebble Beach National Pro-Am as an amateur. Lemmon failed twenty-five times to make the cut.

After the Oscar winner died in 2001, the tournament dedicated a trophy in his honor. The amateur who provides the most scoring help to his pro wins the Jack Lemmon Award.

"Actually, it's named for the guy who helped his pro the least," cracked pro Peter Jacobsen, who partnered with Lemmon from 1981 (when it was called the Bing Crosby National Pro-Am) to 1999. "When Bing passed away, Jack sort of became the unofficial host of this event," Jacobsen told reporters. "Anybody who watched Jack hit that 5-iron fat with mud splashed up in his eye and all the way to his crotch would understand."

During one of the pro-ams, Jacobsen was playing with Lemmon, Greg Norman, and Clint Eastwood at Cypress Point. Lemmon hit a shot on the 16th hole that landed in a patch of thick ice plant growing on the edge of a cliff.

With a crowd of several thousand watching, Lemmon walked over to the edge. "I'm going to let that go," he said.

Eastwood shook his head and said, "Jack, you've got to hit that ball."

Lemmon sighed and, with some trepidation, pulled out his wedge and started creeping over the edge, which had an eighty-foot drop to the rocks below.

"I don't want to see you go off the side," said Eastwood. "Let me hold onto your belt." Then he clutched the belt and braced himself while Lemmon leaned over.

"Oh great," moaned Jacobsen. "Two American film icons are going to fall in the rocks." So he grabbed Eastwood by his belt. Then Norman took hold of Jacobsen's belt. Anchoring this human chain was Norman's caddie, Pete Bender, who held onto his golfer's belt.

Amazingly, Lemmon hit the shot perfectly out of the ice plant and onto the fairway to the cheers of the gallery. But unfortunately Lemmon shanked his next shot into the ocean. Seeing the wayward shot, Jacobsen said, "Jack, that's the best you can do after we risked our lives for you?"

SILENCE IS GOLDEN

During the 1987 Skins Game at the Stadium Course at PGA West in La Quinta, California, Lee Trevino made a hole in one on the 131-yard, par-3 17th hole, which is surrounded by water and rocks and known as Alcatraz.

When Trevino saw his ball roll into the cup for an ace worth $175,000, he raised his club in triumph and then jumped into the arms of his caddie. The hole in one (which, through 2007, no other Skins player has made) left the loquacious golfer speechless.

Skins opponent Jack Nicklaus took advantage of the rare moment of silence from Trevino to note, "Lee, I think that's the first time in my life I've ever heard you shut up."

CLOSE CALL

When golfing, President Warren Harding hated to wait and instead insisted on chasing his ball before his playing partners hit.

One day in 1922, famous sportswriter Ring Lardner was playing with the president. Lardner, who was unaware of the president's impatience, let loose a low screamer and then watched in horror as it missed Harding's head by about an inch.

"Well," Lardner told his caddie, "I tried my level best to make [Vice President] Calvin Coolidge president."

VENUSIAN LOGIC

Playing in an alternate-shot couples' tournament with his wife, Melissa, in 1999, Tom Lehman, the 1996 British Open winner, stroked his 1st-hole tee shot 275 yards down the middle of the fairway.

Melissa then shanked the second shot, leaving the ball one hundred yards from the green. But her husband managed to hit the ball to within fifteen feet of the cup. Then Melissa badly muffed the par putt, pushing their ball twenty feet beyond the hole.

Somehow, Lehman sank the putt and salvaged a bogey. As they walked off the green, he told her, "You've got to do better than that."

Responded Melissa, "Well, you took three shots. I only took two."

TALKING SMACK

Nick Faldo gained a reputation for growing rabbit ears as his game declined. The worse he played, the more frequently his caddie, Fannie Sunesson, admonished the gallery with "Quiet, please!"

At the 1998 Kemper Open, Faldo was having trouble concentrating and was annoyed by the slightest noise or movement. Playing partner Joey Sindelar noticed that Faldo and Sunesson were so testy they were making disparaging comments about the marshals, who were only trying to help them by keeping the spectators quiet.

Soon Sunesson was barking directly at the marshals, claiming that by raising their paddles, which were designed to quiet the crowd, they were distracting Faldo.

On the 6th hole, when the caddie once again chided the marshals for holding up their paddles, Sindelar finally felt compelled to say something to Faldo but decided to keep it light-hearted. He walked over to Faldo and made a crack that his playing partner didn't find funny. Sindelar told him, "Somebody must have paddled you with one of those when you were a kid."

PASSING REMARK

When they reached the 3rd tee at Maplewood Country Club in Bethlehem, New Hampshire, amateurs David Wood and Paul Britton came upon a mixed foursome of two elderly couples on the fairway ahead of them. The foursome signaled for the pair to play through.

"That's okay," Wood said. "We're in no hurry."

"Oh, please, we insist!" said a member of the foursome.

So with all eyes on him, Wood stepped up to the tee and sent his drive screaming into the woods on the right. Not to be outdone, Britton promptly launched his drive an equal distance into the woods on the left. Sufficiently humiliated, the pair motioned to the polite foursome to carry on.

Upon arriving at the next tee, the two golfers spotted the foursome about one hundred yards down the fairway. The elderly couples once again urged the guys to play through. This time, Britton sent a decent drive safely onto the fairway beyond the foursome. But Wood stepped up and drove a foot-high screamer smack into the golf cart of one of the elderly couples. Fortunately for all, the ball then careened down the fairway without harming anyone.

As Wood, with his hat pulled down over his eyes, was passing the couple in the newly dented cart, he heard the woman tell her husband, "See, Harold? You're not that bad."

—from badgolfer.com

ADDRESS CORRECTION

A golfer named Lloyd from Butte Falls, Oregon, was playing golf with a friend and his wife, Kathy, for the first time. Kathy was a sweet middle-aged woman who was golfing horribly.

Lloyd noticed that she would approach her next lie and immediately swing without taking the time to properly address the ball. On a par-4, Kathy was still a long way from the green after her eighth shot when Lloyd approached her. As gently as he could, he told her, "Kathy, have you ever thought about taking the time to address the ball?"

"Oh yes," she replied. "I just called that one a no-good son-of-a-bitch."

—from badgolfer.com

GRAND SLAM

n 1969, while playing a round with Vice President Spiro Agnew, Jimmy Demaret kept wincing at his playing partner's form. Halfway through the round, the former pro told him, "Mr. Agnew, I believe you have a slight swing in your flaw."

FROM BAD to WORSE

PALMER ON THE ROCKS

Arnold Palmer had reached the 17th hole at Pebble Beach during the third round of the 1964 Bing Crosby National Pro-Am. The 218-yard par-3 ran toward the sea to a green flanked by rocks and the Pacific Ocean. It's an intoxicatingly beautiful hole—and an often frustrating one.

To his horror, Arnie hit his tee shot over the cliff behind the green, into shallow water in front of the 18th tee. Back then, the bay and its beaches were played as part of the course. They were not lateral water hazards, which would have allowed a golfer to drop the ball on dry land with a penalty stroke.

(The local rule was later abolished, and the beaches are now considered water hazards.)

As a national TV audience watched in amazement, Palmer stood there, with a curious stray dog behind him, and pondered his shot. Roving TV reporter Jimmy Demaret told viewers the options under the unplayable ball rule: "If he takes the option of dropping behind the point where the ball rests, keeping in line with the pin, his nearest drop is Honolulu."

Palmer gamely flailed away on the rock beach as his ball bounded from one large stone to another. It took him six shots to get the ball off the beach and onto the green in the seventeen-minute televised drama. Arnie then two-putted for a lamentable nine.

Jim Murray, famous columnist of the *Los Angeles Times,* described the scene from the vantage point of his living room TV set: "Palmer . . . was so far out on a moor in the ocean he looked like Robinson Crusoe. His only companions were a dog and a sand wedge. I thought for a minute we had switched channels and Walt Disney was bringing us another of those heart-warming stories of a boy and his dog. But a companion, peering closely, had a better idea: 'Shouldn't that dog have a cask around his neck?'"

PARKING BLOT

L PGA Tour Hall of Famer JoAnne "Big Mama" Carner was at a tournament in which she was determined to show everyone how far she could hit. She blasted her first tee shot and sliced it deep into an adjoining parking lot. So she teed up again and slammed her next drive into the exact same area.

Rather than fly into a rage, JoAnne turned to the hushed gallery and announced, "Well, that lot's full. Let's see if I can park this baby someplace else."

RESOUNDINGLY BAD

A t the 1919 U.S. Open at Brae Burn Country Club in West Newton, Massachusetts, Scottish pro Willie Chisholm and playing partner Jim Barnes reached the 185-yard, par-3 8th hole. Between the tee and the green was a deep ravine with a bubbling brook that snaked its way through large rocks.

Barnes lofted his tee shot onto the green. But Chisholm's ball fell on the steep bank below the green, coming to rest against a boulder. After surveying the situation, the Scot decided to hit it out rather than take a one-stroke penalty for an unplayable lie.

With a firm grip on his trusty niblick (the 9-iron), he swung. The clubhead crashed into the boulder, giving off a few sparks and a sharp ring, and bounced over the ball. The impact sent shock waves jangling through his body. It should have been a warning that perhaps this wasn't the best approach. But the hard-headed Scot tried the same shot again, with the same bone-jarring results.

Now, beyond all reason, Chisholm, acting like a man possessed, began hacking away at the boulder. Sparks darted and rock chips flew, but the ball didn't budge.

From the middle of a wooden bridge that spanned the ravine, Barnes looked down at Chisholm and counted strokes. He marveled that the hickory shaft hadn't broken, but he noticed that the clubhead gained a new dent with each stroke, which totaled fifteen before the ball finally made it to the green, where the flummoxed Scot three-putted.

Not exactly sure how many strokes he had taken, Chisholm asked Barnes, "Do you know my score for this hole?"

Barnes winced and said, "Willie, you took an 18."

Chisholm stared at him in disbelief and said, "Oh, Jim, that can't be so. You must have counted the echoes."

HITTING THE BOTTLE

In the second round of the 1949 British Open at Royal St. George's in Sandwich, England, Irishman Harry Bradshaw sent his drive on the 451-yard, par-4 5th hole into the rough. Imagine his surprise when he discovered that his ball had bounced into a broken beer bottle. The bottle was standing upright with the neck and shoulder broken off and jagged edges sticking up.

Rather than ask for a ruling, Bradshaw chose to play the bottle and ball. He closed his eyes and swung. The bottle splintered into dangerous shards that flew in all directions. But the ball moved only twenty-five yards. Shaken by this unlucky incident, he took a double-bogey 6 on the hole. Eventually he wound up in a playoff, which he lost to South African Bobby Locke.

Officials, reporters, and fellow golfers told Bradshaw that had he sought a ruling on the bottle, he could have treated the bottle as an obstruction and moved it. Under the existing rules, he could have placed the ball on the ground where the bottle had been without penalty.

Said Bradshaw, "If the ball had been in a Guinness bottle, I could not have brought myself to hit it."

IN AND OUT OF LUCK

New York Yankees coach Don Zimmer has never been known as a good golfer. So imagine his playing partners' surprise when he aced the par-3 12th hole at Wentworth Golf Club in Tarpon Springs, Florida, in 2001. Zimmer, one of the roughly 42,000 lucky people each year who score a hole in one, was high-fiving everyone for nailing his first ace.

"Play a new ball and keep your old one for a souvenir," suggested one of his pals.

Riding a surge of confidence, the old coach waved off the advice. "No way!" he declared. "This ball is bringing me luck!"

Moments later, Zimmer chili-dipped his very next shot straight into the middle of the pond and watched it sink out of sight. Zimmer, who wound up scoring a ghastly 135 for the round, turned to his playing partners and said, "See? The ball brought me luck—just not the right kind."

GETTING CLOSER

Champions Tour player Tom Jenkins was playing in a pro-am in Hawaii in 2007, offering encouragement to one of his playing partners who was a real duffer. On a par-5 hole, the amateur hit two good shots, leaving him with a short approach to the green.

"You have a great chance to par this hole," Jenkins said.

Jenkins's caddie, Bob McFadden, consulted his yardage book and told the hacker, "You've got a hundred yards to the hole."

The golfer took a valiant swing. But instead of hitting the ball, the clubhead stuck in the turf, and the player stumbled forward, kicking his ball.

Stifling a laugh, McFadden told the duffer, "Now you've got ninety-nine."

SINGING THE BLUES

Singer Johnny Mathis was playing golf at Moor Allerton Golf Club in Yorkshire, England, with three British companions when he faltered badly on the 8th hole.

He socked his first drive out of bounds. The second tee shot soared over the trees out of sight. His third drive went even farther, but, alas, it too was never seen again.

Muttering to himself, Mathis determinedly teed up another ball, only to send that to bye-bye land as well. His fifth ball tailed off into a bush, but at least it was found.

As his group walked down the fairway, Mathis lagged behind. Suddenly, his smooth, silky voice filled the air as he sang musical scales, ending triumphantly on the highest note. When his playing partners wheeled around in wonderment, Mathis told them, "Thank God, I can still sing."

SPLASHDOWN

Raymond Floyd had a reputation for being one of golf's greatest front-runners. True to form, he had a 4-stroke lead at the turn of the final round of the 1994 Senior PGA Championship at PGA National in Palm Beach Gardens, Florida.

But then, in a few shocking minutes, he plunked two balls into the water on the 15th hole for a quadruple bogey and another ball into the drink at the 17th for a double bogey. The mis-hits led to an 8-shot swing and handed the title to Lee Trevino.

KICKBACK

Several years ago, businessman Joe Mastroianni was golfing with clients at a club in Illinois that required caddies.

At one point in the round, he was faced with a 150-yard shot onto an elevated green. He chose his club and took his stance.

Pointing to a large tree down-range, his caddie shook his head and said, "I think you're lined up to hit that tree."

"No, I'm shooting way right of that big tree," Mastroianni insisted. He went ahead and swung and experienced that satisfying feeling when one strikes the ball just right. He posed for several seconds and then watched in dismay as the ball smacked into the huge trunk of that very tree.

Dismay turned into alarm when the ball rebounded right back at Mastroianni. The caddie hollered, "Watch out!" But the golfer didn't move an inch. Instead, he watched the ball land at his feet and roll dead inside the divot he had made.

"Wow! What a shot!" the caddie exclaimed. "I've never seen a shot like that."

"Well, you're still young," said Mastroianni, patting him on the back, "and I've had years of experience."

—from badgolfer.com

As Floyd's caddie walked from the scoring tent beside the last hole, a youngster asked for a ball to keep as a souvenir.

"We've got none left," said the caddie with a cynical smile. "We left them all in the water."

A MISFIRING FORD

Former President Gerald Ford loved to golf even though he had more than his fair share of wayward shots—especially in pro-ams, when he was the center of attention and the gallery was his unintentional target area.

Bob Hope called Ford "the most dangerous driver since Ben Hur" and noted, "There are forty-two golf courses in the Palm Springs area, and nobody knows which one Gerald Ford is playing until after he has teed off." The comedian once showed up for a round with Ford wearing a helmet.

One year, during the Bob Hope Chrysler Classic, Ford hit a shot wide of the green on the par-3 3rd hole of the Palmer Course at PGA West. The ball took a single bounce off the cart path and landed in a trash can. Moments later, the former president rummaged around until he finally found his ball.

He took a free drop, then muffed his chip shot. Turning to the gallery, Ford pointed to the trash bin and grumbled, "I should have just left the ball in there."

BUGGED BY THE RULE BOOK

Battling for the lead in a tense playoff with Ben Hogan and George Fazio at the 1950 U.S. Open at the Merion Golf Club near Philadelphia, Lloyd Mangrum trailed by only one stroke as the trio approached the green on the par-4 16th hole.

After sighting the line of his putt, Mangrum noticed a gnat resting on his ball. The golfer waited for the insect to fly off, but it didn't. So he used the putter to mark the ball's position, picked the ball up, and blew on it until the offending gnat flew off. Then he put the ball back on the green and drained a fifteen-footer for what he thought was a par. After watching Hogan hole his par putt, Mangrum assumed he was still only a stroke behind.

But Isaac Grainger, chair of the U.S. Golf Association rules committee, informed Mangrum that the golfer had broken a rule that was in place at the time: A golfer cannot lift a ball that is in play under penalty of two strokes. Even though Mangrum was a veteran, he had never heard of the rule. Instead of being down by one, he now trailed by three. With only two holes left, it was too late to catch eventual winner Ben Hogan.

Afterwards, Mangrum tried to deflect reporters' criticism of his ignorance of the rules. "I don't know the traffic regulations of every city I go to either," he said, "but I manage to drive through without being arrested."

SELF-RULE

n one of the early Masters in the mid-1930s, Bobby Jones's father, Colonel Robert P. Jones, was pressed into service as a rules official.

It had rained hard at Augusta the night before the final round, creating soggy fairways. At the 12th hole a player summoned Jones and requested relief from casual water. The colonel asked him where he stood in the tournament.

"Eighteen over," the player answered.

The colonel told him, "Hell, do anything you want," and walked away.

THE DANGER OF GRASS

During the 1992 Swedish Open, Australian Steve Elkington was in a bunker, waiting for his opponent to hit his next shot. Absentmindedly, Elkington reached down, plucked a piece of grass, popped it in his mouth, and began to chew.

A rules official came over and reminded him that it's a one-stroke penalty for touching a hazard. The chagrined golfer nodded and sheepishly explained, "My stomach caused my brain not to work momentarily."

IDENTITY CRISIS

Vacationing amateur golfer Peter Ferlise, of Florham Park, New Jersey, was golfing in 1987 at Florida's Boca West Country Club when he launched a horrible drive onto another fairway.

He figured he wouldn't have any trouble finding his ball because he played with golf balls that had his name printed on them. When he walked toward where he figured his ball had landed, he noticed that a woman was about to swing at it.

"Pardon me, miss, but are you playing the right ball?" Ferlise asked.

She hesitated, then picked up the ball and studied it. "Yes, it's mine," she said. "I'm playing a 'Peter Ferlise.'" Then she put the ball back down, hit her shot, and walked on.

STRIP TEASER

At the Colonial in 1993, Ian Baker-Finch sent an errant shot on the 13th hole to the edge of a water hazard. The Australian, who had won the tournament four years earlier, studied his situation. The ball sat on a muddy bank but was playable.

He knew his nice slacks would get splattered the moment he hit the ball. Because of the high temperatures in Fort Worth, he didn't carry any raingear in his bag, figuring it would be too hot to put on. Not wanting to get gunk on his pants, he did the only thing he could think of: He peeled them off.

In a cap, shirt, and boxer shorts, the unabashed Aussie walked down to the muddy bank while the gallery hooted and hollered good-naturedly. He knocked the ball back onto the fairway, splashing muck on his lily-white legs. Then he cleaned himself off, put his pants back on, and bogeyed the hole.

For the rest of the round, women in the crowd followed him and kept singing out on every shot, "Hit it in the water! Hit it in the water!"

Afterwards, a reporter asked PGA official Duke Butler whether Baker-Finch would be fined for his impromptu striptease. Butler responded, "For what? Lack of a tan?"

NAME SHAME

Famous golf instructor Bob Toski learned to play golf at Northampton Country Club in Leeds, Massachusetts. Before he made it to the PGA Tour as a player, he began competing in small club tourneys in the northeast.

He improved enough to qualify for what was then the biggest tournament of his budding career. Back then he played under his given name, Bob Algustoski. It was a proud moment for the young golfer as he stepped up to the 1st tee in front of a large crowd.

But he turned red from embarrassment when the announcer boomed out, "Now playing, Bob Aglus—Bob Aguss—Oh, hell, play away."

The gallery roared with laughter. From then on, the golfer was Bob Toski.

TEE-HEE TIME

A t the 1965 Los Angeles Open, pro Johnny Pott, who at the time had won three times on the tour and twice played on the Ryder Cup team, stepped up to the first tee.

There, the announcer boomed out this introduction: "Now on the pot, Johnny Tee."

SHIP OUT

G ardner Dickinson, who played on the PGA Tour in the 1950s and 1960s, often was easily distracted when he was ready to putt. (Former CBS producer–director Frank Chirkinian once joked, "Gardner could hear a mosquito break wind two fairways away.")

One time during the San Diego Open in the 1960s, Dickinson balked over a putt three times. Finally, he signaled for tour official Wade Cagle to come over.

"Is there a problem?" Cagle asked.

"Yes," replied the golfer. Pointing to a Navy cruiser on maneuvers off the coast of the seaside course, Dickinson said, "See that battleship out there? You've got to get that boat out of the way."

JIM-JAMS

Entering the final round of the 2001 Senior PGA Championship, Jim Thorpe was tied for the lead with Tom Watson and Bob Gilder.

As Thorpe stepped up to the 1st tee at Ridgewood Country Club in Paramus, New Jersey, the starter introduced him. "Now on the tee, from Heathrow, Florida, please welcome Jim Dent."

There was some nervous laughter among the spectators, who realized the announcer had confused sixty-two-year-old Jim Dent, winner of twelve Senior PGA Tour events, with fifty-two-year-old Jim Thorpe, a four-time winner in his third year on the circuit.

Before the embarrassed announcer corrected himself, a grinning Thorpe said loud enough for the gallery to hear, "Why the hell couldn't he say I was Tiger Woods?"

BUNKER MENTALITY

TAMPERING THE TEMPER

Sergio Garcia wasn't playing well in the second round of the 2006 U.S. Open at Winged Foot in Mamaroneck, New York. On the back nine, he was getting a little desperate because he was in danger of missing the cut. So he swung hard off the 14th tee only to watch his ball curve into the woods.

Anger welling up, the Spaniard was ready to heave his club, but he still had enough control to walk over to a rules official first. "If I throw this driver over those trees, will I get fined?" Garcia asked him.

The official replied, "Yes, you probably would."

"I don't want to see this club anymore."

"Why don't you donate it to charity?"

Garcia, who ultimately missed the cut with a woeful 16 over par, nodded. "Fine," he said, handing over his 3-wood. "Maybe someone else can make good use of it, because I sure can't."

MELTDOWN

Brad Faxon was in third place in the final round of the 1999 GTE Byron Nelson Golf Classic with only a few holes to go. Sadly, he finished bogey, bogey, double bogey, bogey to end up 18th.

After signing his scorecard, the shell-shocked golfer shook hands with Byron and Peggy Nelson and managed to stay polite, but he was slowly melting down. When he returned to his hotel room at the Four Seasons in Irving, Texas, Faxon picked up a chair and started pounding it on the bed in fury.

Then he hurled the chair—and pulled it. The chair slammed into a giant painting on the wall and smashed the frame into a million pieces. In a millisecond, Faxon went from anger to shame. Glass shards were everywhere, and he had to use a sock over his fingers to pick all the pieces off the bed.

The contrite golfer called the general manager of the hotel and asked, "Are you a golfer?"

"Yes, I am. Why do you ask?"

"Well, I was in third place about an hour ago, and now I'm in 18th, and you're one painting short."

When Faxon offered to pay for the smashed painting, the general manager said, "No, that's okay. Like I said, I'm a golfer. I totally understand."

CLUBICIDE

Ken Green, the PGA Tour's bad boy in the late 1980s and early 1990s, was sometimes called Fly by his fellow pros because he threw his clubs as if they were chicken bones headed for the trash can.

Green has claimed he was fined an unofficial Tour record twenty-three times because of his big mouth and hot temper. The golfer, who liked to wear shoes the color of his last name, had a penchant for unceremoniously drowning misbehaving putters. One time, during the 1989 Players Championship, Green was fined $500 by the PGA after he angrily tossed his club into a water hazard. An un-apologetic Green accepted the fine, claiming, "That putter had to die, needed to die. I either give 'em away or they die an ugly death."

MADMAN ACROSS THE GREEN

At the 1968 French Open, Brian Barnes was on the leaderboard early in the second round at Saint-Cloud. But then trouble flared up on the short par-3 8th hole. He bunkered his drive and hit a weak chip shot that left him with a long putt and a short temper.

Swearing under his breath, Barnes stroked an equally bad putt that rolled dead three feet short of the cup. Now seething mad, Barnes tried to rake the ball into the hole like some irate Monte Carlo croupier at the craps table. But it was no dice holing out.

Completely losing it, Barnes turned his putter into a hockey stick and batted the ball back and forth—while it was still moving—and still couldn't knock it into the cup.

He kept swatting the ball while hopping around the green, too infuriated to think about the penalty strokes. He wound up with a disastrous 15.

SWEET SPOT

Craig Stadler was tied for the lead in the fourth round of the 1985 Hawaiian Open at Waialae Country Club in Honolulu. On the par-3 7th hole, his tee shot missed the green and landed in a bunker.

Furious with his drive, Stadler vented his anger by taking his 6-iron out on the closest object to him: the golden pineapple tee marker. Thinking it was plastic, Stadler whacked it hard with his club. Nobody was more surprised than Stadler when it turned out that the pineapple, like all the other tee markers on the course, was real. He juiced the fruit, showering himself, his caddie, a couple of marshals, and several spectators with pieces of pineapple that ranged from chunked to diced to pureed.

"Hey, Craig," shouted someone in the gallery. "Do the same with a coconut and we can make ambrosia!"

Stadler couldn't help but laugh. He regained his composure to shoot 64 and finish a stroke behind winner Mark O'Meara.

Later he told O'Meara, "I'll never look at a pineapple the same way again."

Before Barnes stalked off the green, his astonished marker, who had frantically tried to keep score during the dervish-like performance, wasn't sure of the count. So, with total disregard for his own safety, the marker asked Barnes, "What did you make?"

"You're the marker, don't you know?" Barnes snapped.

The scorer retorted, "Well, when you catch your ass in a buzz saw, it's not too easy to tell how many teeth bit you."

THUNDER BOLT

Terrible-tempered Tommy "Thunder" Bolt heaved enough clubs—mostly putters—in his day to stock a pro shop. It wasn't uncommon to see him putt out with a 2-iron because he had chucked his putter into the drink.

Bolt, the 1958 U.S. Open champion, threw his clubs the way he threw his tantrums: with a style all his own. His face fixed in fury, Bolt would rear back, plant his feet far apart for leverage, and hurl the offending club high in the air, making it spin like a propeller. "I learned that if you helicopter those dudes by throwing them sideways the shaft doesn't break so easily," he once said. "Here's irony for you:

The driver goes the shortest distance when you throw it, the putter the farthest. And here's a tip: Never break your driver and putter in the same round. Oh, and always throw your clubs in front of you. That way you don't waste energy going back to get them."

Because of his club abuse, in 1957 the PGA Tour adopted the "Tommy Bolt Rule," which prohibited the throwing of a club. The day after the rule went into effect, Bolt rocketed his putter skyward because, he explained later, "I wanted to be the first fined under 'my' rule."

Later that same year at the Colonial in Fort Worth, Bolt blew an easy putt on the final hole in front of 15,000 spectators. Playing partner Ed "Porky" Oliver knew that Bolt was seconds away from another angry toss, so Oliver rambled over to the hotheaded golfer, pried the putter out of his clenched fist, and threw it into a nearby pond. He turned to Bolt and said, "I'm just trying to save you a fine."

Another time, Bolt flubbed a short putt that cost him a few thousand dollars. After chewing the grip off his club, he looked skyward and vented his wrath at God.

"Me again, huh?" Bolt thundered. "Why don't you come down here and play me? Come on, come on! You and your kid too! I'll give you two a side and play your low ball!"

WHERE THE SUN DON'T SHINE

Years before he became a respected Illinois prosecutor, Tom Wartowski of Rockford, Illinois, agreed to go golfing for the first time with a friend during a Florida vacation.

The six-foot-two, 240-pound rookie golfer borrowed a set of old clubs that were meant for a much smaller person and headed for an executive course in Delray Beach for what was supposed to be a fun day. After his friend gave him a ten-minute lesson on how to stand and how to hold the club, the two began their round.

It wasn't a pretty sight. Wartowski either topped the ball or, more frequently, missed it entirely. With each flub, his frustration and anger grew. By the 3rd hole, he was through. You couldn't really blame him.

The third and fourth fairways were side by side with only treeless rough separating them. On his final hole, Wartowski's ball was on the left side of the third fairway, about fifty yards from the tee after his second shot. Two golfers in a cart on the fourth fairway nearby stopped as a courtesy so the novice hacker could hit without any distractions.

Wartowski stood over his ball and swung his 5-iron. Whiff. He tried again. Whiff. His neck turning red, he swung a third time. Whiff.

The players in the cart began to snicker, which only added to Wartowski's exasperation, aggravation, and humiliation. Once more, he tried. And once more he whiffed.

One of the players stepped out of the cart and, making a motion as though his pitching wedge were a pool cue, yelled out to Wartowski, "Why don't you try shoving the ball down the fairway, like this?"

The guy then sped off when Wartowski, strangle-gripping the neck of his 5-iron and thrusting it upwards, shouted back, "Why don't I try shoving the club up your ass, like this!"

GONE CLUBBING

In the early 1990s, a group of about twenty guys played every Saturday morning at the Shalimar Country Club in Shalimar, Florida.

Of course, there was always money involved—more than they should have been betting. On one particular Saturday, several thousand dollars was on the line. Steve Wallace and Joe Nacchia were playing well while their opponents, Aaron Talley and Harry Gates, were suffering an off day.

The golfers came to the 390-yard par-4 14th hole, with water bordering the green. All four hit good drives and were within 110 yards of the cup. Talley took out a wedge and hit a shot right on line with the flag, but it came up ten yards short and plunked into the water.

He was so angry he broke the wedge over his knee. Still fuming, he dropped another ball, went over to the cart, and asked Gates whether he could borrow his wedge. Gates handed him the club and watched as Talley smacked a shot that once again was straight and true but, unfortunately, ten yards short. Another splasher.

By this time Talley was so furious that, without thinking, he hurled the club out into the middle of the lake. As the wedge was spinning in midflight, Gates shouted, "Hey, that's my club!"

The wedge was sinking in the water when Talley wheeled around and snapped at his playing partner, "If you can't afford this fucking game, then don't play it!"

LOST CAUSE

During the Chrysler Great 18, a made-for-TV golf event in 1993, John Daly lost his temper—and his clubs.

On the 18th tee at Pebble Beach, Daly told playing partner Fuzzy Zoeller, "If I hook this ball in the water, I'm going to throw this damn driver in with it."

"You don't want to do something crazy like that," said Zoeller. "You've had enough trouble this year." (At the beginning of the year, Daly, a self-confessed alcoholic, underwent a rehabilitation program. Near the end of the season, at the Kapalua International in Hawaii, Daly walked off the course after blowing an easy putt on the 11th hole and was suspended by the PGA Tour.)

Sure enough, Long John hooked his drive into the Pacific Ocean. Seeing how fuming mad Daly was, Zoeller held out his hand and asked, "May I?"

Daly handed him the club. Zoeller then tossed Daly's driver twenty-five yards out into the water.

Moments later, Daly botched several more shots along the way to the hole and pitched two more clubs—his 2-iron and 8-iron—into the surf. When he finally finished the hole, the disgusted Daly gave his golf bag and the remaining clubs to a little girl in the gallery, saying, "You could do better with them than I can."

ON THE REBOUND

n the late 1940s, pro Henry Ransom ran into trouble at Cypress Point's infamous 16th hole, a 220-yard par-3 where the tee shot must clear a spit of ocean and a rocky cliff. His drive stalled in a headwind and smacked into the cliff below the green, falling onto the beach.

Three times he wedged shots near the top of the cliff, and three times the ball rolled back down. On his next shot, the ball ricocheted off the rocks and struck him right in the stomach. Ransom then ordered his caddie to pick up the ball. The golfer stalked off, muttering, "When the hole starts hitting back at me, it's time to quit!"

PUTT TO SHAME

Depression-era golfer Ky Laffoon, winner of ten PGA Tour events, became so frustrated with his putting at the 1935 Jacksonville Open that after walking off the 16th green, he began choking his putter.

Then, still squeezing it at the neck of the shaft, he trod ankle-deep into a creek, shoved the club under the water, and screamed, "Drown, you poor bastard, drown!"

Another time after his putter let him down, Laffoon stormed off the course at the end of a tournament and waited in the car for fellow golfer Sam Snead, who was going to drive with him to the next stop on the tour.

As Snead loaded the clubs in the trunk, he noticed that Laffoon had tied his putter to the back fender. "Why did you do that?" Snead asked.

"That putter of mine deserves to be humiliated because of the way it behaved today," answered Laffoon. And so the club bounced along the back for about three hundred miles. When they finally arrived at their destination, there was nothing left but a jagged shaft.

JUST ONE OF THOSE FLINGS

Comedian George Gobel and actor Jack Albertson agreed to let a lone golfer join them for a round at Hillcrest Country Club in Los Angeles in 1952.

The newcomer had a terrible temper, and whenever he hit a bad shot, he hurled a club in disgust. Gobel couldn't believe how far the clubs flew.

Toward the end of the round, Gobel shanked a shot so badly that he was fit to be tied. To vent his anger, he stormed over to the other golfer's bag, whipped out a 3-iron, and flung it into the rough.

"Why in the hell are you throwing my club?" the outraged golfer demanded.

"Because," replied Gobel, "your clubs are used to it."

INSULT to INJURY

LET IT BEE

Actors and friends Bill Murray and Will Smith were playing a friendly round of golf in 2007 when Smith stopped to sign autographs for fans who had come out to watch them play.

Suddenly, Murray began running up and down the fairway, screaming and flapping his arms. Smith laughed at the spectacle and told the fans, "He does this whenever I get all the attention. He wants you to ask for his autograph too."

Murray, who was still yelling, ripped his shirt off. Only then did Smith realize that the comedian wasn't joking. Something was wrong. Smith raced over to his friend and discovered that Murray had been stung on his back by a bee.

Leading Murray back to the clubhouse to treat the sting, Smith apologized for not taking the comedian's raving more seriously. Cracked Smith, "I guess I took your actions the same way I take your golf—as a joke."

NOW *THAT'S* A SKINS GAME

Before he became a TV golf analyst, Gary McCord tried to make a name for himself on the PGA Tour. He did, but it had little to do with his golfing prowess. He made people laugh, often inadvertently.

For instance, take the time Gary was playing in the 1984 Memphis Classic. On the 15th green, he bent down to line up a putt when he heard a loud rip. His pants had split from the seam by his belt in the back all the way under his legs to his crotch. That was bad enough. Even worse, he wasn't wearing any underwear because he hadn't bothered to do his laundry that week.

In a panic, he dropped his putter and put both hands over his caboose because he was basically mooning the gallery. Facing the tittering spectators, the red-faced Mc-Cord slowly backed away, keeping his legs tightly together.

The fastest way out of this embarrassing predicament, he thought, was to put on his rain pants as quickly as possible. So he told his caddie, "Go in my bag and get my rain pants—fast!"

The caddie shook his head and said, "Gee, I'm sorry. But since it's such a hot day and there's little chance of rain, I left your rain gear behind to lighten my load."

"That's just great," McCord muttered. He turned to his playing partner, Andy Bean, and asked whether he could borrow his rain pants. The sympathetic golfer agreed, and McCord breathed a sigh of relief—until Bean's caddie admitted that he too had left behind the rain gear.

Now McCord was desperate. He grabbed his caddie's towel and draped it around his waist so that he looked as if he were wearing a diaper. Spotting another group of golfers on the adjoining fairway, McCord hustled over to them, related his mortifying plight, and begged for help. It was just his luck that one of the members of the group was Peter Jacobsen, a kindred spirit, although a much better player than McCord.

"Tell you what," said Jacobsen. "I'll let you use my rain pants."

"Oh, thanks, man, I really appreciate it," said McCord.

"But," added Jacobsen with a mischievous grin, "it's going to cost you twenty bucks."

At that point McCord was willing to pay any price to save himself from further humiliation. He agreed to pay him on the 19th hole and finished the round in Jacobsen's rain pants.

Back at the clubhouse, McCord paid up, saying, "It was not a pleasant or hygienic experience. I just want to put this whole episode behind me."

FLUB CLUB

Willie Nelson was playing with long-time golf partner Darrell Royal, the former University of Texas football coach, at the singer's Pedernales Golf Club in Spicewood, Texas.

Early in the match, Nelson asked Royal, who was in the cart, to give him his 2-iron. Royal pulled it out of the bag and threw it to the singer. But Nelson had been distracted by a shot from another golfer that landed near him. The flying club slammed into Nelson's head and knocked him nearly unconscious.

Royal rushed over to his buddy and worriedly asked, "Are you all right?"

The still dazed singer said, "Am I bleeding out the ears?"

Royal shook his head.

Nelson slowly picked himself up off the ground and said, "Then I guess I'm not hurt."

FLOP SHOT

While playing in a pro-am event at the Nestle Invitational at the Bay Hill Club in Orlando in 1992, Curtis Strange was hit in the head by a stray shot from one of his amateur partners, who was trying to punch the ball out of the trees.

The two-time U.S. Open winner dropped like a flop shot. Strange was dazed and bleeding but suffered no permanent injury. When one of his other playing partners saw that Strange would be fine, he joked with the pro, "Luckily it hit you in a nonvital organ."

DOWN UNDER

n the first round of the 1992 Honda Classic at the Weston Hills Golf & Country Club in Fort Lauderdale, Florida, John Huston hooked two drives into the lake on the par-5 7th hole.

Hitting five, he sprayed his next drive right off the fairway. Huston, who had won the tournament two years earlier, was so furious that he helicoptered his Wilson Whale driver into the pond that had claimed his first two balls.

When he realized what he had done, Huston raced to the edge of the water. Seeing that the club was still floating, he took off his shoes, rolled up his pants, and waded in after it. As he was about to reach his driver, the golfer fell off an unseen shelf at the bottom of the pond and disappeared below the surface.

Surprised that Huston was nowhere in sight, playing partner Mike Hulbert dashed to the bank and saw Huston's hat floating on the water. Just then Huston popped up, swam to the edge, and crawled out with his driver.

When Hulbert stopped laughing, he told Huston, "Hey, it's not so bad. You got your driver back, and you've gained a new nickname."

"What's that?" asked the soaked golfer.

"Swamp Thing."

SHANKS FOR THE MEMORY

One day in 1967, when renowned golf instructor Butch Harmon was an assistant at Winged Foot Golf Club, he was standing opposite the man to whom he was giving a lesson on the practice range.

Suddenly a golf ball hit Harmon right in the rear. He turned around and saw that the culprit was Chuck Mercein, a running back for the Green Bay Packers, who was hitting practice balls about ten feet away. Even though Mercein had his back to Harmon, the player somehow managed to accidentally hit the ball between his own legs and caught the instructor squarely on the backside. It was a unique reverse shank.

"That may have been the worst shot I've ever seen," Harmon told Mercein.

"But you didn't see it," contended the player.

Harmon nodded and said, "Okay then, it's the worst shot I've ever *felt*."

EM-BARE-ASSING

While playing golf in Pennsylvania, Geoff Toonder putted out and walked back to the cart. As his playing partner, Dr. Bob Oristaglio, sank his putt, Toonder suddenly jumped out of the cart and dropped his pants. He had suffered a bee sting on his rear and asked Dr. Oristaglio to get the stinger out.

The sight of a man kneeling next to his playing partner's bare butt bemused the golfers playing behind the twosome. The group rode up to the two men and asked one simple question: "What was the bet?"

AND AWAY WE GO!

Comedian Jackie Gleason loved golf so much, he had his special cart customized to look like a miniature Mercedes. It featured a telephone, television, refrigerator, two-way radio, and, of course, a wet bar. He drove it all over his home course at Inverrary in Lauderhill, Florida, sometimes even into the bunkers.

HEADSTRONG

"**W**ith reference to the reported world's record rebound of a golf ball from the head of a Scotch caddie which appeared in the home golfing papers, I beg to inform you that whilst playing the 7th hole at the Premier Mine course [in Transvaal, South Africa] on 28th September, my ball struck a native caddie (who was standing 150 yards away at the side of a tree just off the line of the fairway) on the forehead just above the right eye. The drive in question was one of those so dear to a golfer, a hard, raking shot. The ball rebounded back in a direct line seventy-five yards (distance measured). Strange to relate, but beyond a slight abrasion of the skin, the native was not affected at all. Therefore, you will readily observe that the record of the Scotsman is easily outclassed."

—Edward Stanward, writing to *Golf Monthly,* 1914

One day in the 1970s, he was playing with a friend and parked the golf cart near a pond. While the golfers were walking toward the green, the cart slipped out of gear and rolled down the bank and into the water.

"Oh, my God, Jackie!" shouted his playing partner. "Your golf cart just went into the pond!"

The unflappable "Great One" glanced over at the submerged cart and sighed, "Well, there go my cigarettes."

JOHNNY ON THE SPOT

During a practice round at the 1975 Jackie Gleason's Inverrary Classic in Lauderhill, Florida, Lou Graham, that year's U.S. Open champion, entered a portable restroom precariously placed on the lip of a canal.

When he tried to leave, he found that the door latch had jammed. He yelled for help, but no one heard him. Then he got the brilliant idea to step up on the seat and kick at the latch with his golf shoes. He gave it a few hard thumps but noticed that the outhouse began teetering like a bowling pin. Another kick, and the portable john would have tumbled into the canal.

"Oh, great," Graham muttered out loud to himself. "I can see it now on the evening news: 'Golfer drowns in outhouse.'"

Once the wobbly john settled down, he came up with a better idea. He took off his shoe and beat the latch open. After telling his playing partners what had happened, he mused, "I wonder if Johnston and Murphy would want to do an ad on how a pair of their golf shoes saved a pro's life."

A BAD TIME

Tiger Woods won the second of his three straight amateur titles at the 1995 U.S. Amateur Championship at Rhode Island's Newport Country Club. Lost in Tiger's triumph was the heartbreaking story of a fellow competitor.

At the players' dinner the night before the tournament, rules official Tom Meeks told all golfers to remember which of two courses they were playing on and from which tee they were starting. The next day, Meeks received word that a player from Montana had shown up at the wrong course. An all-points-bulletin was put out, and when the player was notified, he caught a ride on the back of a spectator's motorcycle that wove through terrible traffic to get to the right course.

By the time he arrived at the correct tee, his group had already left. He was so late that Meeks had no choice but to disqualify him. It nearly broke the official's heart because he discovered that the player had missed qualifying for the tournament the previous year by a single stroke.

When Meeks told the golfer he had been disqualified, the young man looked at the official a long time and said, "Mr. Meeks, do you mind if I lie down here and cry for a minute?" Meeks nodded. Then the golfer went to the corner of the tee, curled up, and sobbed.

Turning to a fellow official, Meeks whispered, "It's all I can do to not go over there and cry with him."

LEAP OF FAITH

When Evel Knievel wasn't risking his life by jumping his motorcycle over a row of buses or other large obstacles, he was usually golfing.

In the mid-1970s, he golfed a lot at Rivermont Golf and Country Club in Alpharetta, Georgia. The club's signature hole is No. 17, a 174-yard par-3 featuring an elevation change measuring 110 feet from the tee to the green below.

The cart path runs steeply downhill with a series of hairpin turns. A careless cart operator could go zooming off the cliff.

Knievel's golfing buddies pointed out that if a cart gathered enough speed it could fly over the ledge and land where the path resumed farther down the hill. For days they goaded the daredevil to make the jump in his cart. He knew better.

But one afternoon Knievel arrived at the 17th tee in a foul mood because he hadn't been playing well. After his tee shot missed the green, he was steaming mad and decided he would try to make the jump in the cart.

Halfway down the hill, he thought that perhaps this was a mistake. He found out how unstable a three-wheel golf cart is when it becomes airborne. But it was too late. Fortunately, he made a perfect three-point landing. Because the tires were like basketballs, the cart bounced several times. When Knievel regained control of the cart and stopped it at the bottom near the green, his wife chewed him out. He couldn't blame her. She had been in the passenger seat the whole time.

A CAUTIONARY TALE

Roger Maltbie, then a rookie on the PGA Tour, was delirious when he won the 1975 Pleasant Valley Classic, his second win in a row. The first prize of $40,000 was the biggest payoff of his young career.

Usually when a pro wins a tournament, he is handed a large dummy check made out of cardboard. But this time, Maltbie received a real check. He stuffed it in his pocket, which was already bulging with $600 in cash that he had brought to the tournament. Feeling happy and rich, Maltbie chose to celebrate his good fortune at a bar called T.O. Flynn's in Worcester, Massachusetts. He pulled out the cash, threw it on the bar, and announced to everyone in the place, "Let's have fun! Let's get drunk—on me!"

Taking himself up on his own words, Maltbie quaffed a few too many shots and closed the place up. The next morning, he woke up with a hangover. Trying to clear his head, he wondered, *Where am I? What did I do last night? Where have I been?* Then it dawned on him: *Man, I won the tournament. I won two in a row.* It was flooding back to him.

The first thing he wanted to do was buy a newspaper and read all about himself. He put on his pants and reached into his pocket for some money. No coins, no cash, and no check. He sat down on the bed and tried to reconstruct exactly what happened the previous night. *Just where was I?* Finally, he remembered. *That's it! T.O. Flynn's.*

Hoping against hope that some honest soul had found the lost check, Maltbie called the bar. A member of the cleaning crew answered the phone. "I was a patron in there last night, and I lost a check in your establishment."

"Are you okay? You sound pretty nervous."

"Well, it's a pretty big check."

"How much is it for?"

"Forty thousand."

"Forty thousand! No, we don't have anything like that. I'd know if we did."

Fighting hard to quash a panicky feeling in the pit of his stomach, Maltbie then called Cuz Mingolla, the general chair of the tournament.

"I've got a problem," Maltbie told him. "Last night I lost the check."

Mingolla laughed and said, "Don't worry about anything. We'll stop payment on it and send you another check, so relax."

Maltbie sighed with relief and hung up. But then he thought, *I don't have any cash. I can't get out of town.* So Maltbie called Mingolla back. "Can you send your guy over with a $39,000 check and $1,000 in cash so I can get out of town?"

"Sure, no problem," replied Mingolla with a chuckle.

After receiving the replacement check and cash, Maltbie got a call from the manager of Flynn's. The manager said the cleaning lady had been vacuuming the floor when she noticed a balled-up piece of paper. She picked it up and was shocked to see it was a check for $40,000. She promptly turned it in.

"Do you mind if I photocopy the check so I can frame it and put it up over my bar?" asked the manager.

"Be my guest," said Maltbie. "Man, for a while there, I was in really bad shape. I had no check and no cash."

"What happened to all that money you had last night?" the manager asked.

"The six hundred dollars? That was all drunk up."

ALL the BETTOR

BOTTOM DOLLAR

Long before Charlie Sifford became the first African American to play—and win—on the PGA Tour, he caddied for touring pro Clayton Heafner, who won seven times in the 1940s and 1950s and finished second in the U.S. Open in 1949 and 1951.

As a teenager who grew up in the same city as Heafner—Charlotte, North Carolina—Sifford learned a lot about the finer points of the game just by watching the pro. Although Heafner was a superb golfer, he had a hair-trigger temper and seemed angry all the time on the course. More than once, he would fire Sifford somewhere on the front nine and then rehire him a few holes later on the back nine.

Despite his bouts of rage, Heafner believed in fairness and would let his young black caddie play a round with him on Mondays, ignoring the stares and ugly comments from racist southerners. By the time Sifford was sixteen, the caddie felt confident enough to take Heafner on for money. Sifford held his own against the pro.

But one day, the caddie, who had only a few coins in his pocket, made the mistake of playing him for $2. When Heafner closed him out, Sifford apologized and said, "I'm sorry, but I don't have the two dollars."

"You don't, huh?" growled the hulking, strong pro. Heafner grabbed Sifford, picked him up, carried him over to a water hazard and threw him in. Shouted Heafner, "Never play for more money than you have in your pocket!"

And Sifford never did.

ON THE BALL

Davis Love III had won a bet from European Tour player Darren Clarke, who promised to pay up later. For some reason Clarke forgot about the 100-pound ($157) wager. During a practice round at the 2003 British Open at Royal St. George's Golf Club, Love spotted Clarke at the practice range about fifty yards away. So Love wrote the amount he was owed on a golf ball and then chipped it so close that it nearly struck the startled Irishman on the head. The ball served its purpose. Clarke paid up.

STAR STRUCK

One of the Hollywood couples rock legend Alice Cooper most likes to play with is Michael Douglas and wife Catherine Zeta-Jones. Douglas has a 16 handicap; Catherine, 25. "I've taken some money off Michael Douglas," Cooper told a reporter. "But I only play with him so I can play with Catherine."

Talking about the time he first met Zeta-Jones, Douglas said he was dazzled by her beauty and talent. But when he found out she was an avid golfer, that made her irresistible. Recalled Douglas, "When she said, 'I like to play golf too,' frankly it brought tears to my eyes."

PAYING HIS OWN WAY

n the early 1950s, when Jerry Barber was trying to make a name for himself on the PGA Tour, he played practice rounds with the best players for money. He believed that to be a good tournament player, he needed to learn to handle the pressure. The only way to prepare for that was to play for an amount he could barely afford to lose.

Long before he won the 1961 PGA Championship, Barber habitually lost money to Sam Snead, who was at the top of his game at that time.

After watching Barber pay off Snead yet again after losing another practice round, fellow golfer Doug Ford said, "Jerry, what the hell are you doing? There's no way you can beat Sam Snead. He's the best player in the world. What are you thinking?"

Jerry said in a matter-of-fact way, "If you're going to attend the university, you've got to pay the tuition."

FAIR WEATHER FRIEND

Doug Ford, winner of the 1955 PGA Championship and the 1957 Masters, spent the winters in his home in Connecticut. The blustery, cold weather made it difficult to keep his game sharp, but he tried to tough it out and played until it snowed. Usually, he went several weeks without swinging a club.

To get ready for the Tour, he went to Los Angeles to play with California golfers who loved to gamble. Invariably, Ford was so rusty that he lost big money to them because it took him a few weeks to play himself into shape.

But one year, the northeast had a freakishly warm winter, which allowed Ford to play every day in December. So when he showed up in Los Angeles and played his California buddies, he cleaned up. They poured money into his hands daily.

Finally one of the golfers asked Ford, "Why are you playing so well?"

Replied Ford, "You need to start reading the weather reports."

ODDBALL

Eccentric Canadian golfer Moe Norman was leading the 1963 Saskatchewan Open by three strokes when he reached the green on the last hole.

He was putting for an easy and inconsequential birdie. But Norman wanted to put more pressure on himself by making the score closer. So, Norman being Norman, he deliberately putted his ball into the bunker.

As he walked over to the hazard, he noticed two men standing in the front of the gallery. It looked as if the blood had drained from their shocked faces.

After Norman got up and down for a bogey to win by two strokes, he walked over to the pair and said, "You two seemed awfully upset when I putted into the bunker."

"That's for sure," one of them said. "We had a huge bet on you to win."

"Sorry that I scared you," Norman said.

"Why did you do that?" the gambler asked.

The golfer replied, "I needed the variety."

GETTING SNOWED

Daredevil Evel Knievel loved to play golf for money. And he simply couldn't resist making bets with Thomas Preston Jr., better known to the world as gambler extraordinaire Amarillo Slim.

The notorious gambler, who made a fortune making proposition bets, once beat Minnesota Fats at pool using a broomstick. He whipped tennis champ Bobby Riggs at Ping-Pong playing with a skillet and beat Knievel in golf using a carpenter's hammer as his only club. (Unbeknownst to the losers, Slim had spent hours practicing with the unorthodox equipment.)

One time when Knievel was appearing in Dallas to make a jump, he had drinks with Amarillo Slim. Naturally, the gambler offered Knievel a wager. "I bet you that you can't break 80 at Preston Trail [a golf club in Dallas] tomorrow," Slim said. At the time, Knievel was a 6-handicapper and had played the course, so he believed he had an excellent chance at winning that bet. The stakes: $10,000.

When Knievel woke up the next morning, he was dismayed to see that 3 inches of snow had covered the ground, and the course was closed. There was no getting out of the bet. Slim had been careful to stipulate "tomorrow," with no questions asked.

The daredevil wrote him a check for the $10,000. "I have no problem with it whatsoever," Knievel told Slim. "If you're going to be a sucker, be a quiet one. Nothing's worse than a guy who loses fair and square and then whines about it."

BREW-HAHA

Golf buddies Rick Fetherolf and Joe Manausa, of Tallahassee, Florida, have an annual tradition of giving up their beloved beer for a month. Because the two pals usually imbibe vast amounts of the precious brew, they have chosen February, with its fewer days, as the perfect month to go on the wagon and lose a few pounds.

But for years, Fetherolf was the first to fall off of the wagon before the month ended. For his failed effort to out-last Manausa, Fetherolf received a great deal of ragging from their mutual golfing friends.

So he was determined that 2007 would be his year. As February was drawing to a close, both men had steadfastly laid off the suds. Manausa conceded to friends that his pal might actually make it through the entire month without touching a beer. Determined not to let that happen, Manausa hatched a diabolical plan on the golf course.

With help from another golf buddy, Roy Barineau, Manausa set the trap during a golf outing at Golden Eagle Country Club on February 28. An empty beer can was secretly filled with diet soda. Barineau placed the beer can in Manausa's golf cart, making certain that Fetherolf would see it.

Barineau was paired with Fetherolf as they set out to play golf with Manausa and other friends. During the round, Manausa drank from the can, which Barineau pointed out to Fetherolf.

"Joe, are you drinking a beer?" Fetherolf asked.

"Hey, Rick, it's the last day of the month," said Manausa. "We made it!" Manausa hoisted the beer can and took another swig.

A huge grin spread across Fetherolf's face. "The day isn't over. That means I finally held out longer than you." Turning to his playing partners, Fetherolf crowed, "I beat Joe! I beat Joe!" To celebrate outlasting his golfing buddy for the first time, Fetherolf drank his favorite beer and downed it with glowing satisfaction.

Over the next few holes, he kept bragging to the others how he had finally bested Manausa. On the 13th hole, Barineau had heard enough and announced to Fetherolf that he had been tricked. When Fetherolf learned that he once again had failed to outlast Manausa, he got so mad that he double bogeyed the next three holes, costing him the match.

CAN'T-LOSE BETS

Chi Chi Rodriguez has always enjoyed a friendly wager on the golf course.

Once in 1966 at the Dorado Beach Country Club in Puerto Rico, he closed out his playing partner, a New Yorker named Ross, for a healthy sum on the 17th hole.

At the final tee, Rodriguez made Ross a proposition: "I'll give you a chance to get even. I'll bet everything on this last hole. I'll give you two strokes if you give me one throw."

Ross, a three-handicapper, readily agreed. They both hit the seaside green on the par-4 18th with their second shots. Ross was fifteen feet from the hole; Rodriguez was twenty feet.

Smiling confidently, Ross said, "Okay, take your throw now, Chi Chi."

"I plan to do just that," Rodriguez replied. He calmly walked over to Ross's ball, picked it up, and threw it onto the beach.

A few years later at the Doral Country Club in Miami, Rodriguez was conducting a golf clinic when one of his students, an Irishman named Jerry, challenged him to a long-distance driving contest. "You can't out-drive me," Jerry boasted.

The five-foot, seven-inch, 135-pound Puerto Rican sized up the big galoot and figured Jerry would be an easy mark. "I'll let you hit a drive and a wedge shot," Rodriguez said, "and I'll bet that you still won't be able to catch up to my drive."

Jerry took the bait, believing the wager would be impossible to lose. Hitting first, he swung so hard that he popped the ball up.

"I want to win this fair and square," Rodriguez said. "Go ahead and hit your drive again."

This time Jerry's ball exploded off the tee and soared 320 yards. There was no way, Jerry thought, that Rodriguez could come close to matching that drive. And even if by some fluke he could, Jerry still had another shot with his wedge.

Rodriguez teed up his ball, gazed at Jerry's ball in the distance, and shook his head in resignation. Then he turned around 180 degrees—and whacked his ball in the opposite direction about 250 yards. Said a grinning Rodriguez, "Now let's see you catch up to that!"

IN THE POCKET

Two years before he joined the PGA Tour full time, Jim Thorpe played in a big money game in 1977 with amateur Brian Stavely at East Potomac Park in Maryland.

Several gamblers backed the golfers in what turned out to be a contest about racial pride as well as $5,000 in wagers. The black bettors put their money on Thorpe, an African American, and the whites bet on Stavely, a young white golfer.

The gamblers followed the two in their nine-hole match, which Thorpe eventually won because of a wayward drive. The golfers had been dead even going into the 8th hole when Stavely hit his tee shot deep into the rough. Everyone looked and looked, but no one could find his lost ball.

"That's odd," Thorpe told Stavely. "I didn't think your ball drifted so far off that we can't find it."

Moments later, one of the gamblers who had bet on Thorpe came over to him and whispered, "He'll never find his ball."

"What do you mean?" asked Thorpe.

The gambler replied, "I got his ball in my pocket."

TITANIC RETURN ON INVESTMENT

Golf hustler Titanic Thompson, whose real name was Alvin Thomas, once played a wealthy rancher in a 1935 game with $10,000 at stake.

Thompson and the rancher came up to the 18th hole all even, and both golfers laid up short of the green on their second shots. However, the rancher's ball landed in a sand trap. Before the rancher reached the bunker, Thompson whipped out a $10 bill, gave it to his caddie, and whispered, "Run up there and drop this in the trap."

Moments later, after the rancher entered the bunker, he reappeared waving the $10 bill and shouting, "Look what I found in the trap!"

Thompson shook his head sadly and cited an official rule that was in force back then that said a golfer could not remove anything from a bunker, not even a rake, until after his shot. "Gee, I'm sorry," he told the rancher, "but that'll cost you a stroke. You lie three."

The hustler won the match—and the $10,000—by virtue of that one penalty stroke.

GROWING UP

C rafty veteran Sam Snead was playing a practice round with eighteen-year-old South African rookie sensation Bobby Cole at Augusta National before the 1967 Masters. Cole, the 1966 British Amateur champion, and Slammin' Sammy were playing $5 Nassaus.

When they reached the 510-yard, par-5 13th hole, an azalea-lined dogleg to the left, the fifty-four-year-old golfer pointed to the tall loblolly pines on the left and said, "You know, Bobby, when I was your age I could drive my ball over those trees."

Taking the comment as a challenge, Cole smacked a drive that he hoped would clear the trees. Instead, it pinballed around in the upper branches, never to be seen again.

Cole shook his head and said, "Man, I can't hit over those trees. How did you do it?"

Snead smiled and said, "When I was your age, those trees were only twenty feet high."

DRIVEN TO DISTRACTION

ong before LPGA star JoAnne Carner was inducted into the World Golf Hall of Fame, she established a reputation as a long-ball hitter. She simply couldn't resist trying to out-drive her opponents.

One day, as in many tournaments, she was paired with Mickey Wright, who could also hit it far. On the first tee Wright said, "JoAnne, please, let's not get into a driving contest." But on the 5th hole, Wright let loose and out-drove Carner by thirty yards. So on the next hole, Carner blasted her drive twenty yards past her opponent.

Their driving competition went on for several holes, both of them bombing away and both spraying their tee shots all over the golf course. Finally, with both of them out of contention, Wright whispered to Carner, "What do you say we play closest to the pin, a penny a hole."

Carner rolled her eyes and said, "Why didn't you suggest that in the first place?"

HOLDING the BAG

GOLF SHOOS

NBA Hall of Famer Bill Russell was playing in a foursome with Davis Love III in the final round of the 2001 AT&T Pebble Beach National Pro-Am. At six-feet-ten and 220 pounds, Russell, a twelve-time All-Star center who led the Boston Celtics to eleven championships in his thirteen years in the league, was an imposing figure on the course.

Love's caddie, John "Cubby" Burke, noticed that Russell had big feet. In fact, the caddie had never seen such huge golf shoes on a person before and knew they could mark up the green. With Davis on top of the leaderboard, Burke deliberately and repeatedly got in Russell's way whenever the hoops legend walked toward the cup. The caddie was afraid Russell's clodhoppers would louse up Love's line.

Throughout the back nine, Burke kept Russell away from the hole by picking up his ball for him and bringing it to him. The caddie did a great job of preventing Russell from stepping anywhere near the cup.

Once victory was in hand, Love told Russell, "You haven't been boxed out like this since you were playing with the Celtics, have you?"

CATCHING FIRE

The tension mounted as rookie Jerry Pate reached the 17th tee in the final round of the 1976 U.S. Open at the Atlanta Athletic Club. He was locked in a three-way struggle with Al Geiberger and Tom Weiskopf, who were playing in front of him.

While waiting for the pair to putt out, Pate stood next to his caddie, John Considine, and his bag. Pate leaned slightly on the bag, crossing his hands and resting them on the headcovers of his woods.

Considine nervously lit a cigarette and watched the other golfers. Just then, Pate jerked and shouted, "Ouch!"

He shook his hand, thinking he had been stung by a bee. But when he looked, Pate discovered that Considine was so uptight that the caddie wasn't paying any attention about how he was holding his cigarette—which was burning the back of the golfer's hand.

Pate began laughing, which loosened him up. One hole later—the final hole—Pate fired a 5-iron from the rough on a bank above his feet 195 yards to two feet from the cup and sank the putt to win the Open.

"See?" Considine told his thrilled golfer. "I lit a fire under you."

CLOSE ENOUGH

Caddie Lynn Strickler, who worked for several great golfers such as Curtis Strange, Ben Crenshaw, and Fred Couples, had an off week one time in the late 1980s, so he carried the clubs for Payne Stewart at the MCI Heritage Classic at Harbour Town Golf Links in Hilton Head, South Carolina.

Like most caddies, Strickler had been giving Stewart the yardage estimates. In the middle of the second round, the golfer said, "Lynn, I've got to ask you a question. How come all your numbers end in zero or five?"

Answered Lynn, "I either round them up or round them down. If it's 162, it becomes 160. If it's 163, it becomes 165."

"Why aren't you more exact?" Stewart asked.

The caddie shrugged and said, "I just don't think you guys are that good."

TO TELL THE TRUTH

Huey Lewis of Huey Lewis and the News, one of the most popular bands of the 1980s, had missed participating in the AT&T Pebble Beach National Pro-Am only three times from 1986 through 2006.

The native San Franciscan is the first to admit that he sings much better than he golfs, having a two-decade-long run of errant shots, blown putts, and lost balls.

In the 2004 event, Lewis watched his drive on the 1st hole at Spyglass Hill sail outside the ropes and into the gallery. As several spectators formed a semicircle around the ball, Lewis sized up his predicament and turned to his caddie and friend Deacon Lewis (no relation).

"Five-wood or 3-iron?" Huey asked.

"Five-wood," the caddie replied.

"Well, I don't hit the 5-wood very well."

"You don't hit the 3-iron very well, either."

YOU SHOULD SEE HIM WHEN HE'S MAD

Herman Mitchell toted Lee Trevino's bag from 1977 to 1994. For years, the two bantered back and forth on the course. Mitchell, a huge man who weighed more than 300 pounds, towered over the five-foot, seven-inch golfer and often playfully chided Trevino when he wasn't playing well. Trevino was quick to fire back with good-natured barbs.

During a tournament in which he suffered several bad bounces, Trevino was cranky and verbally riding Mitchell more than usual. After misreading a putt and settling for a bogey, Trevino took another potshot at his caddie and angrily tossed him the putter.

As the two left the green for the next tee, a woman in the gallery asked Mitchell, "Does he always treat you this way?"

"No, ma'am," the caddie replied. "Today is one of his better days."

PARTING SHOT

Bob "Bullet" Burns was toting the bags for volatile South African Fulton Allem during the 1996 MCI Heritage Classic at Hilton Head, South Carolina. Allem, not the most popular golfer with caddies because of his penchant for firing so many of them, was having a tough second round. Falling farther back in the pack, he hit a series of wayward shots that left his blood boiling.

The struggling Allem was playing so badly midway through the round that he fumed to Burns, "Man, if this keeps up, I'm going to feel like breaking something."

Without batting an eye, Burns said, "How about breaking par?"

The only thing a Tour pro hates worse than an incompetent caddie is an insolent one, especially one who mocks him with the truth.

"Very funny," Allem said sarcastically. And then he fired Burns.

NOT IN HIS JOB DESCRIPTION

On the final hole of the 2006 British Open, Tiger Woods calmly sank the putt to win the championship, his first major victory since the death of his beloved father, Earl Woods. Still mourning the loss, Tiger broke down and sobbed.

He embraced his loyal caddie, Stevie Williams, and began showering the caddie's white duds with tears. It was a touching moment on the green.

But as Tiger continued crying like a baby, Stevie pushed him towards the golfer's wife, Elin, saying, "Here, you deal with this."

A BURGER WITH TEE, PLEASE

Irish golfer David Feherty had been playing a practice round at St. Mellion, Ireland's notoriously rugged course, for four hours (which, he often told friends, was like spending four days anywhere else).

While waiting on the 16th tee, Feherty became hungry and asked his caddie to get him a hamburger, which he did. Before the pro could take a bite, it was his turn to tee off.

Knowing that his caddie loved to eat and would take a bite or two, Feherty didn't want to hand him the burger. So when he stepped up for his tee shot, Feherty pinned the burger to the ground with a tee and hit his shot off it.

"Why did you do that?" asked his caddie.

"I wouldn't mind if I lost my ball," Feherty replied, "but I certainly would mind if I lost my burger."

DON'T ASK, DON'T TELL

Dow Finsterwald, winner of the 1958 PGA Championship, was among the favorites to win at the 1960 U.S. Open at Cherry Hills Country Club in Denver.

But during the first round, Finsterwald was off his game. To make matters worse, he and his caddie weren't on the same page. The relationship grew testier with each hole. Finally, the golfer couldn't take it anymore and fired the caddie on the 16th hole.

It happened when Finsterwald asked the caddie for his opinion on what club to use.

"Why ask me?" replied the caddie. "You've asked me two times already and paid no attention to what I said. So pick your own goddamn club!"

LUSH COURSE

U pon arriving on the Monterey Peninsula to make his debut at the Bing Crosby National Pro-Am in 1969, actor Jack Lemmon received a message stating that his hired caddie would be unable to make it. So Lemmon hurried off to the Pebble Beach caddie barn to find a replacement.

He looked around the caddie pen and spotted an older guy with a big, heavy overcoat. To Lemmon, the bag-toter looked like he'd been lugging clubs for a long time and probably would be a big help, so the actor hired him.

But by the end of the round, Lemmon told a tournament official that he needed to find another caddie. "What happened?" asked the official.

"I pick him up at Pebble in a car I had rented and we head for Spyglass," Lemmon said. "His breath is so strong my eyes start to water. It's 8 A.M., and he's smashed.

"Well, on the first tee I hit a pretty good 3-wood, take a bow for the gallery, and start walking down the fairway, still carrying that 3-wood. I'm on top of the world. Next thing, I turn around and my caddie is gone. He's searching for my bag. Lost it on the first tee. Finally, he finds it and comes rumbling down the fairway, lurching and stumbling. About a hundred yards off the tee, on a piece of perfectly flat ground, he slips. My clubs fly out of the bag and he's flat on his ass.

"Then, on the 2nd hole, I hear this tinkling, like jingle bells. I don't know what the hell it is. Then, the sun comes out, and off comes that big coat, hitting the ground like a 10-ton rock. He had pint bottles stashed away in the lining, four or five of them clanking together on the bottom!"

"Jack," said the official, "you hired one of the great lushes of all time."

"Well, he's driven me to drink."

KEEPING HIS DISTANCE

In the early 1960s few of the rank-and-file pros on the PGA Tour had regular caddies. Typically at each tournament, a caddie was assigned to a golfer. Sometimes the bag-toters were good, and sometimes they were bad.

Journeyman touring pro Bobby Brue thought he had been given more than his share of incompetent caddies. So on one of the Tour spots in 1963, he slipped $10 to the caddiemaster, hoping he'd get a caddie who knew what he was doing. The golfer was given a young, eager, bright-eyed caddie.

When they reached the first tee, Brue asked him, "How far is it to the 1st hole?"

With one eye closed, the caddie gazed down the fairway for several seconds and then replied, "Oh, about three blocks."

THE BREAKING POINT

Caddie Lance Ten Broeck couldn't stand it any longer when his golfer, Jesper Parnevik, missed his sixth putt inside of five feet with a new putter during the 2000 MCI Classic in Hilton Head, South Carolina.

The caddie, who had talked Parnevik into using the putter in the first place, realized something had to be done. If not for his lousy putting, Parnevik would have shot a spectacular opening round. (He wound up shooting 70 despite his woes on the green.)

Ten Broeck held up the putter and asked the golfer, "Do you mind?"

Parnevik shook his head. Then with great flourish, the caddie snapped the shaft over his knee.

"We got a lot of bad karma out of that thing," said Ten Broeck, a former Tour player before picking up the Parnevik bag. "It deserved the death sentence."

ASK AND HE SHALL DECEIVE

Sam Snead was playing the par-5 16th hole at Firestone Country Club in Akron, Ohio, on a windy day when his second shot splashed into the lake in front of the green.

"How far to the green?" he asked his caddie.

"Well," the caddie answered, "yesterday I caddied for Jay Herbert in a practice round and he hit an 8-iron."

Snead grunted, pulled out the 8-iron, and swung. The ball plopped right in the middle of the lake. He was furious. "You mean to tell me that Jay Herbert hit an 8-iron from here?" he testily asked the caddie.

"Yes, sir, he sure did."

"Where'd his shot land?" Snead demanded.

"Oh," said the caddie quite innocently, "Mr. Herbert hit his ball in the lake too."

DAMN CLEVER

British golfer Harry Vardon, one of the sport's first superstars and winner of six British Opens, played in knickers, dress shirt, tie, and jacket. His fame grew in

WAY OUT OF LINE

In the 1954 British Amateur Championship at Muirfield, England, American Frank Stranahan infuriated the caddies because he refused to take their advice. In fact, he fired a bag-toter after each of the first three rounds for arguing with him over club selections.

Things didn't get much better with his newest caddie in the fourth round. Midway in the round, Stranahan was at the tee of a hole where the green was hidden by a high ridge. He sent the caddie to the top of the ridge to line him up in the direction of the flag. When the caddie reached the spot, he waved, and Stranahan hit directly over him. Thinking he made a fine shot, the golfer was shocked when he reached the ridge. The caddie had lined Stranahan up so that the ball landed in a thick patch of ferns.

Seeking revenge for the way Stranahan treated his buddies, the caddie dropped the golf bag at Stranahan's feet and headed for the caddie shack, saying, "Now, sir, if you think you know so much about golf, let's see you get yourself out of there."

1900 when he toured the United States and won dozens of exhibitions, matches, and also the U.S. Open.

He was also a big hit throughout Europe and often competed against his brother Tom. Although Harry was the better of the two at golf, Tom was a master practical joker.

At the French Open one year, Tom, who spoke fluent French, arranged for an attractive young woman to caddie for Harry. The caddie didn't speak English, and Harry didn't speak French, but she had an engaging smile, and she almost always seemed to know what club to hand him before he asked.

Early in the round, Harry struck an approach shot that landed less than a foot from the pin. He turned to the caddie and said, "Now that's a good one."

She smiled at him and said, "Damn fluke."

Somewhat annoyed, Harry tapped the ball in for a birdie. A few holes later, he once again landed his approach within easy putting distance for a birdie. When he looked at his caddie for an approving smile, she gave him one, adding, "Damn fluke."

In fact, that's all she ever said the entire round, and only when he made an exceptional shot. By the time he finished the round, Harry was really annoyed with her.

After signing his scorecard, Harry met Tom, who asked, "So how did you like your caddie?"

"She was all right, but she obviously doesn't think highly of me as a golfer."

"Hmm," said Tom, breaking out into a big grin, "she must have been a damn fluke."

Only then did Harry figure out that Tom had taught the French girl to say "damn fluke" whenever Harry had hit a good shot.

YOU'RE NO HARRY VARDON

Joe Horgan was the dean of American caddies in the first half of the twentieth century and greatly admired English golfer Harry Vardon.

One time Horgan, who worked at the Westchester Biltmore Club in Rye, New York, was caddying for a pro with a big ego. The golfer landed in a trap but then hit a remarkable recovery dead to the pin. The pro turned to the caddie and said, "What do you think of that shot, Horgan? Could Vardon have gotten out the way I did?"

Horgan replied with a snit, "Get out? Mr. Vardon would never have gotten in!"

NOW THAT'S A THOUGHT

A visiting golfer at St. Andrews was having an absolutely miserable round when he hit his third shot into the infamous bunker guarding the green on the Road Hole. "What do I do now?" he asked his caddie.

"Well, sir, the Jigger Inn is just down the road," the caddie said. "I think we should go there, have a wee one and rethink the whole bloody thing."

MAX AND MAD MAC

Englishman Max Faulkner, winner of the 1951 British Open, was considered somewhat of an eccentric because he wore brightly colored plus fours with matching shoes. Also, he sometimes stood on his head in the middle of a round so the blood would flow to his brain.

In keeping with his oddball image, he had a caddie known as Mad Mac, who wore a raincoat but no shirt. When asked to read a putt, he used a pair of binoculars without lenses.

Mad Mac liked booze as much as golf, if not more. One time, the caddie consumed a bottle of brandy and collapsed by the side of the green. Faulkner dragged him behind a gorse bush and left him to sleep it off, playing the round without a caddie.

Nevertheless, the golfer often put his trust in Mad Mac, although the golfer did a double take when, responding to Faulkner's request for a read on the green, the caddie advised, "Hit this putt slightly straight, sir."

TIP WAS TOPS

Arnold Palmer met famous caddie Tip Anderson at the 1960 British Open at St. Andrews.

However, their first practice round together was a calamity. Palmer was playing with Roberto DeVicenzo in winds that gusted up to fifty miles an hour. Palmer, his frustration building with every hole, finally announced at the turn that he wanted to quit.

Anderson would not hear of it. "C'mon, stop yer cryin'," the veteran caddie admonished the world's best golfer at the time. "Ye've come all the way to St. Andrews to win the Open."

Palmer agreed and finished the round, shooting an un–Palmer-like 87. At one point during the round, Palmer reached in his bag and pulled out a 6-iron. Anderson shook his head and said, "Now what in the world are ye gonna do with that?"

The two clicked during the tournament, but Palmer finished one stroke behind winner Kel Nagle, who took nine fewer putts. However, with Anderson toting his bags, Arnie won the next two British Opens, first at Royal Birkdale in England and then at Troon in Scotland.

In 1964, when Palmer didn't compete in the British Open at St. Andrews, Anderson caddied for Tony Lema on Arnie's recommendation. Lema beat Jack Nicklaus by five strokes. Afterward, Anderson liked to needle Palmer, telling him, "Ye won two Open Championships, but I won three."

HAZARD A GUESS

Ever since it was founded in 1894, Portmarnock Golf Club near Dublin, Ireland, has been considered one of the finest links courses in the world. And over the years, their caddies have been known for their wry sense of humor.

An American once found himself in one of Portmarnock's deep pot bunkers. After taking three full swings, the golfer threw his hands up in despair because his ball remained in the bunker. At that point, the caddie asked for the

HEADS UP

Overwhelmed by the aura of St. Andrews, an American visitor was playing horrible golf on the Old Course. For seventeen holes he kept jerking his head up to see where his ball had gone and consequently kept topping it.

On the 18th tee he muffed his drive. It veered straight into the Swilcan Burn, which meanders across the 1st and 18th fairways and provides the only water hazard on the Old Course before emptying into the North Sea. The golfer half-jokingly told the caddie, "Now that my ball is in the burn, throw the clubs in there as well. In fact, I might as well throw myself in and drown."

The caddie, who throughout the dismal round had offered nothing but words of encouragement, could no longer contain himself. With no regard for the tip he was about to lose, the caddie told him, "Ye'll never manage to drown yerself. Ye'll never keep yer head down long enough."

club because he wanted to show the visitor how to finesse the ball out of the sandy bunker.

The caddie took three swings and, like the American, failed to get the ball out onto the fairway. With the air of a touring pro, the caddie emerged from the bunker, returned the club to the golfer, and said, "There, that's what yer doing wrong."

HAIR LINE

Singer Bing Crosby was an excellent golfer and attempted to qualify for the British Amateur Championship at St. Andrews in 1950.

Crosby arrived several days early and enlisted a dour elderly caddie to help him get in a few practice rounds on the fabled Old Course. The entertainer's first round was simply awful, but the caddie kept his mouth shut and didn't utter a single sarcastic crack, for which he and his fellow Scottish club carriers were so famous.

In his next practice round, Crosby showed some modest improvement compared with the day before. Midway through the round, he asked his caddie, "So, do you think I look a little better today?"

"Aye," the Scot replied. "Ye've had a haircut!"

TAKE YOUR TIME

Australian actor Oscar Asche was playing a particularly bad game of golf on a Scottish course. After an uncharacteristically good shot, Asche told his caddie, "I'm sure you've seen worse players than me out here."

The caddie, an aged Scot, didn't say anything. Thinking the caddie had not heard him, Asche repeated his remark.

"I heard ye afore," the caddie said. "I was thinkin' if indeed I had seen anyone worse."

LOST IN PARADISE

While playing on the Queen's Course at Gleneagles, Scotland, years ago, U.S. Golf Association official George Smith and his wife arrived at the 13th hole, which called for a blind tee shot across a ravine.

Smith's drive landed on the fairway on the other side, but Mrs. Smith's drive sailed off to the right into a well-nurtured stand of heather. Her caddie dutifully hacked his way into the thick foliage and searched for the ball. After several minutes passed, Mrs. Smith declared the ball lost and decided to play another.

As she headed back toward the tee, she noticed that her caddie was still searching determinedly through the heather. "You can stop looking for the ball now," she told him.

"It's not the ball I'm looking for, Mum," the caddie replied. "It's yer clubs I've lost."

OUT of BOUNDS

LEARNING THE ROPES

In his first Masters in 2001, Chris DiMarco, like all Masters rookies, was in awe of Augusta National. When he went into the locker room for the first time, he took off his shoes and put them on the bench. As soon as he did, one of the attendants came up to him, frowned, and said, "Here at Augusta, we do not put our shoes on the bench."

Embarrassed by the faux pas, DiMarco gulped and said, "Okaaay. I better write that one down."

WAIT 'TIL NEXT YEAR

R oger Maltbie was thrilled when he arrived at Augusta National in 1976 to compete in his first Masters.

He was one of the early golfers to arrive because he wanted to soak it all in and enjoy every minute of this experience. Back then, players were assigned caddies by the club. He was given Porky Dent, a cousin of player Jim Dent.

Maltbie registered with officials, got his locker, walked outside the clubhouse, and saw a fleet of green Cadillacs. He asked Porky, "What are those cars doing there?"

"Those are courtesy cars for the players to drive," the caddie replied.

Maltbie walked back inside the clubhouse and told an official, "I see you have a fleet of these courtesy cars. Is it possible for me to get one of them?"

The official shook his head and said, "No, they've all been reserved."

"I looked at all the literature and stuff you sent us, and I didn't see anything about courtesy cars," Maltbie countered.

The official sniffed and replied, "Well, if you ever come back, you'll know."

WHAT A RELIEF

When golfers step up to the urinals in the men's locker room at Rock Creek Golf Club in Jacksonville, North Carolina, they can find some comfort in the words of a sign on the wall. It says, "This is the only place on the golf course where no one is trying to change my grip or stance."

IT AIN'T KOSHER

The Maidstone Club is a private, extremely exclusive seaside country club in the village of East Hampton, New York.

Reportedly, back in the 1950s, Groucho Marx played a round there as a guest of one of the members. The comedian loved the course and asked his friend about the possibility of joining the club.

His friend blushed and said, "I'm sorry, Groucho, but the club won't accept you as a member because you're Jewish."

Without missing a beat, Groucho said, "My kids are only half-Jewish. Can they at least play the front nine?"

HE SHOULD'VE HAD THE SOUP AND SALAD

When Australian Steve Elkington was paired up against Colin Montgomerie at the 1995 World Match Play at the Wentworth Club in Surrey, England, the press billed it as a chance for the Scotsman to seek revenge. A few months earlier, Elkington had beaten him in a playoff at the PGA Championship.

Before the second round action at Wentworth, Elkington was having lunch with his wife, Lisa, in a quiet corner of the castle-like clubhouse. Across the room at a large table, Montgomerie was playing host to more than a dozen people who were scarfing down the fabulous buffet.

Elkington watched as Montgomerie got up and went over to the buffet, which featured a huge replica of the clubhouse made out of custard. "Crikey," Elkington said to Lisa. "Monty just wiped out the whole west side of the custard clubhouse. I think he took part of the locker room too."

Lisa glanced over her shoulder and then told Elkington, "Isn't that nice of him? He scooped up all that custard to share with the people at his table."

Moments later, Elkington said, "Well, I'll be damned. Monty just ate the whole thing by himself. You know what that means, don't you?"

"No, what?"

"There ain't a man alive who can eat that much custard and beat me."

He was right. Elkington won the match, 2 and 1.

A WOOD FROM WOODS

Tiger Woods won the 2006 British Open at Hoylake's Royal Liverpool without hitting into a single fairway bunker. By using only irons and no woods, he led the field in driving accuracy and missed just eight of fifty-six fairways.

The striking fact led playing partner Nick Faldo to ask Tiger for an audacious item in the traditional post-tournament gift swap. Usually players give signed balls and gloves. Instead, Faldo asked Woods whether his son, Matthew, could have Woods's driver. Tiger gladly gave it to the young man.

"Why not?" Faldo said to fellow golfers. "Tiger wasn't using it."

DIRECT FROM THE HORSE'S MOUTH

Word has a way of getting around fast when someone has a great day on the golf course. In 1985, one husband got so tired of hearing his better half brag about her super round that he posted a notice on the bulletin board at the Rancho Sierra Golf Course in Lancaster, California.

The note stated: "My wife played her best round of golf last Sunday. Would those who have not heard about it, please phone [her number] for full details of every shot!"

RETURN TO SENDER

When comedian Bob Hope turned ninety in 1993, one of his presents was a basket of ninety golf balls from the exclusive Valencia (California) Country Club, where he was a member. Each ball was inscribed, "Happy 90th, Bob."

Hope thanked general manager Ken Kikuchi for the gift and said, "Now when I hit one in the water, the fish will know who to send it back to."

THE LONG AND THE SHORT OF IT

For decades, Jackie Burke Jr. has taught the finer points of golf to amateurs and pros alike.

America's grand golf sage is in the Hall of Fame for his seventeen Tour victories, including the Masters and PGA Championship in 1956 and a 7–1 Ryder Cup record. Since his playing days, he's been a successful coach for stars such as Phil Mickelson, Hal Sutton, and Steve Elkington.

One day in 2000, Burke was in the clubhouse at the Champions Golf Club in Houston (which he co-founded with Jimmy Demaret), talking to some members about how he once helped a duffer. "When I taught at Metropolis Country Club in New York, there was a fellow who shanked chip shots, nothing else," Burke recalled. "The man smoked a pipe, and after a lot of thought, I began placing his best pipe just outside his ball. He was terrified of hitting the pipe with the toe of the club, you see, and I cured him quick."

One of the members who had been listening to Burke's story left the room. An hour later the guy returned and placed his pipe, which was shattered to bits, in front of Burke, and said, "Your tip doesn't work for long irons."

SAME OLD, SAME OLD

In 2001, seventy-year-old Betty Dunham won the women's championship at the Onawa (Iowa) Country Club for the nineteenth time. The victory came forty-three years after she won her first club title.

With Dunham's victory, the amateur golfer had won club championships in each of six decades. At the presentation of the trophy, she told everyone, "I dedicate this victory to all the old bags out there who love to play golf."

FOR WHAT IT'S WORTH

Guitarist and singer-songwriter Stephen Stills, best known for his work with Buffalo Springfield and Crosby, Stills, Nash & Young, loves to golf.

But not everyone is thrilled to see a long-haired rocker on the golf course, especially on one of the venerated centuries-old links in Scotland. Stuffy old members of a course near Edinburgh were peeved when Stills, his hair in a ponytail, prepared for a round with an elderly man who couldn't have cared less what his fellow Scots thought about his famous playing partner.

As the pair headed toward the first tee, Stills heard loud grumbling from some of the members, complaining that a rock musician had no business on such a distinguished course. They tittered with glee when he hit an ugly shot off the tee. But Stills recovered and played well on the cold, rainy day.

On the 18th tee, with the condemning eyes of the grouchy members watching from the clubhouse, Stills crushed his drive 260 yards uphill. Then he nailed a 6-iron within three feet of the pin and sank the putt for a birdie.

His Scottish partner shook his hand and said, "You see those sonofabitches who've been giving you dirty looks because they don't like you or your ponytail?"

Looking up at the clubhouse patio, Stills nodded.

"Well, you just screwed them in the arse," the Scotsman said. "Good for you, laddie! I'm proud of you."

HE'S GOT A POINT

A good friend of Bobby Jones loved to golf but carried a high handicap. One day in Atlanta, the pal came into the clubhouse and eagerly told Jones about an eagle 2 the duffer had made on a par-4 hole.

"What club did you use for your second shot?" Jones asked.

"A 4-wood," the friend answered.

"A 4-wood?" Jones said in astonishment. "Why, I've never used more than a 9-iron on that hole."

Responded the friend, "You ever make a two?"

SKIRTING THE ISSUE

A sign erected outside a County Kerry course in Ireland in 2001 has left some women golfers perplexed and their male counterparts hopeful. It reads, "Trousers are now allowed to be worn by ladies on the course. But they must be removed before entering the clubhouse."

BRAVE ADMISSION

Amateur Floyd Slasor of Phoenix, Arizona, was on Moon Valley's mammoth par-4 10th green, 127 feet away from the pin, when he putted the ball firmly in the direction of the flag. Incredibly, the ball dropped in for what was one of the longest measured putts ever recorded.

After Slasor finished his round, club members had already heard of the remarkable coast-to-coaster. The golfer politely accepted their congratulations in the clubhouse, then felt compelled to make an embarrassing admission.

"It wasn't for a birdie," he told them. "It was for an eight."

OH, DEERE!

When Mark Hensby won the 2004 John Deere Classic, he was especially thrilled because it was his first tournament victory on the PGA Tour.

At the ceremony immediately after the win, the tournament sponsor presented him with the money and a traditional gift for this event. He was given the keys to a shiny new John Deere lawn tractor.

Accepting the keys, Hensby laughed, saying, "I live in Arizona. I hope it can mow dirt."

WRONG NUMBER

Ed "Porky" Oliver, winner of eight PGA events in the 1940s and 1950s, enjoyed playing Cypress Point—except for one time.

In the 1953 Bing Crosby Pro-Am, the five-foot, nine-inch, 240-pound pro found disaster on the seaside 16th hole. After drilling five shots into the ocean, Oliver carried the water, but his ball landed in tangled ice plant, a nemesis with fleshy, spiky leaves. He chopped around in the foliage until he finally holed out with an unsweet 16.

Word spread fast around the course and clubhouse about his calamity on the 16th. When Oliver finished, there was a message waiting for him in the clubhouse. An attendant walked through the bar, announcing, "Porky Oliver, please call long-distance operator sixteen. That's operator sixteen."

DECLAWING A CRAB

When South African pro Bobby Locke came to the United States in 1947, he won six of the thirteen tournaments he entered. In fact, in his two and a half years on the PGA Tour, he won eleven events and finished in the top three in thirty.

Locke built his success around his outstanding putting ability, coining the phrase "You drive for show but putt for dough." Wearing his trademark knickers, white shoes, and stockings, Locke played the game at a slow and deliberate pace, which annoyed many American pros. What really irked them was getting beat by a foreign player who was taking home so much of the prize money.

One day in the clubhouse, a pro who resented Locke's success walked up to the South African and snidely told him, "You have a weak left-handed grip."

Locke shrugged it off, saying, "That's not a problem. I take the checks with my right hand."

PRESSING MATTER

After making his first PGA Tour cut in two years at the 1999 Honda Classic at the TPC at Heron Bay in Coral Springs, Florida, Mark McCumber told friends in the clubhouse that finally playing in a tournament on the weekend felt great.

But, he admitted, because of his unexpected showing, he was now faced with a pressing matter: his wardrobe for days three and four.

"I'll have to go shopping," he told them. "I don't think I have any more clean shirts."

THOSE WERE THE DAYS

In 2000, Tiger Woods had one of the greatest years in golfing history.

He won three consecutive majors—the U.S. and British Opens and the PGA Championship—among nine Tour victories. Setting or tying twenty-seven Tour records, he had record earnings of $8,286,821 and a nonadjusted scoring average of 68.17. Tiger finished the year with forty-seven consecutive rounds of par or better and completed all twenty events under par. He also won the PGA Tour and PGA of America player of the year honors.

Over a clubhouse lunch, a writer asked him whether this was his best year ever.

"No," Tiger replied. "When I was eleven, I had straight A's, won thirty-two junior tournaments, had two recesses a day, and had the cutest girlfriend in the whole school. Everything has been downhill since then."

HARD TO DUPLICATE

Zeppo Marx, of the famous Marx Brothers, liked to hold court in the clubhouse bar discussing his favorite sport. One day, as fellow golfers gathered around, he gave his opinion of the most difficult shot in golf: "The hardest shot is a mashie [a 5-iron] at ninety yards from the green, where the ball has to be played against an oak tree, bounces back into the sand trap, hits a stone, bounces onto the green, and then rolls into the cup. The shot is so difficult I have only made it once."

AN EITHER–OR SITUATION

Dave Marr, winner of the 1965 PGA Championship, later turned into a TV golf analyst for ABC. He became friends with NFL great Frank Gifford, who spent more than twenty-five years in the broadcast booth, announcing Monday Night Football for ABC.

At Gifford's insistence, Marr tried to help him improve his golf game, but it was a tough task. Finally after another frustrating lesson on the practice range, Marr bought Gifford a drink in the clubhouse bar and bluntly told the NFL

Hall of Famer, "Frank, either you have to get better soon or quit telling people I'm your teacher."

WHERE TO NOW?

Claude Harmon Sr., head pro at Winged Foot Golf Club, was the last club professional to capture a major title, winning the 1948 Masters by five strokes. He taught his sons to play golf, and they all became top golf instructors.

One day, he was working on the swing of his teen-age son Billy on the driving range. The young man was in a groove and was stroking the ball exceptionally well. At least he thought so. But he was irked because his father remained silent and offered no praise. Finally Billy asked him, "What are you thinking about, Dad?"

"I'm thinking about P. T. Barnum and the Ringling brothers," Harmon replied.

"What about them?"

"Barnum and his guys travel to Africa and get young elephants for their shows. They spend time with them and train them. Those they can't train, they ship back to Africa."

"So what's your point, Dad?"

Harmon shook his head and said, "I've got no place to send you."

SWING THOUGHTS

Warning to hackers during a golf lesson: Don't ask a pro about your game unless you're ready for the painful response.

A duffer asked Ken Venturi, "How do I put more distance between myself and my shots?"

Replied Venturi, "Hit the ball and run backwards."

Englishman Ted Ray, winner of the 1912 British Open and the 1920 U.S. Open, was renowned for his power, which he tried to teach to his golf students. When asked by a student how to obtain more distance, Ray replied, "Hit it a bloody sight harder, mate!"

The great Byron Nelson once studied actor Jack Lemmon's swing. His analysis? "My God, he looks like he's beating a chicken."

BATTY BANTER

PGA player Pearl Sinn (Bonanni) drew stares when she headed to the practice range with a Louisville Slugger at the 2000 ShopRite LPGA Classic at the Marriott Seaview Resort Bay Course in Galloway Township, New Jersey.

"What are you doing with that bat?" asked fellow pro Liselotte Neumann.

"It's great for strengthening and swing velocity drills," replied Sinn.

Eyeing her warily, Neumann said, "It looks odd having a baseball bat at the practice range."

With a wink and a smile, Sinn said, "Okay, the truth is I plan to use my bat to knock out the competition."

"Well, you can leave me alone," said the Swede. "I'm not playing that well."

TURNING IT AROUND

Famous golf writer Charles Price tried to play the Tour back in the late 1940s but was having little success. Sitting in the clubhouse bar one day, he asked pro Clayton Heafner, "Why can't I play golf?"

Heafner eyed Price's slender five-foot, nine-inch, 135-pound frame and said, "Have you ever noticed that most of the young guys who come out here are pretty big? Most of them are built like a truck driver. And did you notice they can all putt? Most of them have a touch like a hairdresser. Well, the trouble with you is, you're built like a hairdresser and putt like a truck driver."

PRACTICE RANGE HAZARD

Long before he became commissioner of the PGA Tour, Deane Beman was a young phenom who qualified for the 1955 U.S. Open at the Olympic Club in San Francisco when he was just a junior in high school.

Beman, who later won two U.S. Amateur Championships, convinced his teachers to let him skip classes so he could spend the extra days practicing for the biggest tournament of his life. A few days before the Open, he arrived on the practice tee with his bag of old golf balls. (Back then, golfers brought their own practice balls.)

He was hitting the used, shoddy balls when Ben Hogan arrived and set up a few yards away. Hogan's caddie opened a large box of Titleists and dumped the sleeves of shiny new balls onto the ground.

Moments later, another pro, Bo Wininger, took his place on the other side of Beman. Wininger carefully opened his shag bag, and two dozen new balls rolled out.

While the pros began practicing, Beman continued to hit his odd collection of balls, many of them scarred and cut. Using his 4-wood, Beman whacked a severely cut ball that took off with a loud *pfffft*.

Wininger glanced over his shoulder at Beman, looked down at the sad bunch of balls at the teenager's feet, and asked him, "Son, aren't you afraid one of those things is going to explode?"

SO *THAT'S* THE PROBLEM

A novice named Sheryl J. was out at the driving range after purchasing her first set of clubs. She had never played before but was determined to take up the game.

As she was whacking away from the practice tee, she looked around and wondered why everyone else at the range was driving the ball so much farther then she was. She turned to the man next to her and complained, "I am striking the ball as hard as I can but I can't get my ball to go as far as anyone else."

He figured out her problem right away. "Lady," he said, "quit using your putter and you might be able to put some air under the ball."

—from badgolfer.com

WHAT'S LUCK GOT TO DO WITH IT?

Gary Player, three-time winner of both the Masters and British Open, was practicing in a bunker in Texas one day when a good old boy with a big wad of money and a hat to match stopped to watch.

The diminutive South African promptly holed a shot from the sand.

The Texan wasn't that impressed and said, "You get fifty bucks if you knock the next one in."

Player, who at the time was one of the best golfers in the world, chipped the next ball, and it rolled straight into the cup.

Still not awed, the Texan said, "You get one hundred bucks if you hole the next one."

Amazingly, Player sank that bunker shot for three in a row.

As the Texan peeled off the bills, he told the golfer "Boy, I've never seen anyone so lucky in my life."

Retorted Player, "Well, the harder I practice, the luckier I get."

ON the ROPES

A SORRY FAN

When Scotsman Colin Montgomerie was paired with Phil Mickelson at the 1997 U.S. Open at the Congressional Country Club in Bethesda, Maryland, a fan cheered when Montgomerie hit a poor shot.

Angered by the outburst, the golfer confronted the spectator, who meekly said, "I'm sorry."

"No, you're not."

"Yes, I am. I'm sorry."

"No, you're not."

"Yes, I'm sorry."

"No, you're not."

Finally the fan admitted, "You're right. I'm not."

CLUELESS

Actor Samuel L. Jackson enjoys signing autographs for kids, but only if they are polite and say "please." At the AT&T Pebble Beach National Pro-Am, Jackson was walking near the ropes by a large group of kids, all of them waving their programs for him to sign. But none of them were saying "please," so the actor figured it was time to enforce his rule.

Speaking loudly so the whole gallery could hear, the actor asked the kids, "What are you supposed to say?"

The kids didn't answer. Instead, they continued waving the programs. So Jackson said again in a more stern voice, "What's the magic word?"

Still none of the kids responded. The actor was ready to walk away when one of the bigger kids, with a look of total frustration on his face, started mumbling loudly. Only then did it dawn on Jackson that these kids were from a local school for the deaf on a field trip to see the stars golf.

As the adults shot dirty looks at Jackson, the actor signed all the kids' scorecards and didn't stop until his playing group fell a hole behind.

LOOK GOOD, PLAY BAD

Steve Ballesteros—winner of the 1980 and 1983 Masters and the 1979, 1984, and 1988 British Open—turned fifty in 2007 and made his debut on the Champions Tour at the Regions Charity Classic in Birmingham, Alabama. Nearly three decades had passed since he won his first green jacket at the age of twenty-two and became the youngest champion of a major in the twentieth century.

During his first round on the Champions Tour, Ballesteros heard a fan yell, "You look every bit as good today as you did when you were winning majors."

The Spaniard, who finished the tournament tied for 77th, smiled and said, "Thank you for the compliment. I only wish you were right!"

EASIER SAID THAN DONE

Jim Furyk has been known to pull a spectator out of the crowd during a practice round if the fan boasts a little too loudly something like, "I can hit that shot."

One time before the British Open, Furyk was playing a practice round with Steve Stricker and Lee Janzen while a small but vocal gallery followed them. On one hole, Stricker and Furyk each had a ball in the same area off the green. Stricker went first and hit his chip shot to within eight feet of the cup.

As Furyk was ready to make his shot, someone in the gallery said, "I can hit one better than that."

Furyk stepped away, turned to his caddie, and said, "Throw me a ball." After catching it, he dropped it near his ball and then handed the fan a wedge and challenged, "Let's see what you've got."

The cocky fan went up to the ball, swung, and laid sod over it.

While the gallery laughed, Furyk told him, "Not as easy as it looks, is it?"

SCORING BIG LAUGHS

Comedian George Lopez was paired with eccentric pro Jesper Parnevik at the 2004 AT&T Pebble Beach National Pro-Am. Lopez, who considered himself a fashion plate in a color-coordinated outfit, looked at the pink snakeskin vest and red pants that his playing partner was wearing and cracked, "Jesper, you look like a kid's playroom exploded."

Turning to the gallery, Lopez announced, "We are like Starsky and Hutch. We're going to nauseate the competition into submission."

Paul Stankowski and actor Andy Garcia rounded out the foursome. "Andy and I are the first two Latinos to play together here," Lopez joked with the crowd. "They were going to put Robert Gamez in our group, but three Latinos is a gang."

At the 17th hole, Lopez backed away from his approach. Pointing to a fellow Hispanic who was pushing a loud lawnmower beside a home along the fairway, the comedian told the gallery, "You'd think the Mexicans would try to *help* me!"

FAN SUPPORT

Jerry Kelly stood over his ball at the 18th tee at the TPC at Sawgrass in the third round of the Players Championship in 2004. He was on the leaderboard and in the last group of the day on a sunny afternoon in the Jacksonville suburb of Ponte Vedra Beach, Florida.

Kelly was only nanoseconds from taking his club back to begin his swing when some jerk from the gallery broke the silence by yelling "Noo-nan!" The obnoxious fan was referring to Danny Noonan, the young caddie in the 1980 classic film *Caddyshack*.

Kelly managed to stop his swing in time and glare at the boorish spectator. Then the golfer swung and went on to par the hole.

Afterwards, Kelly told reporters how annoyed he was by the loudmouth. "That was pretty pitiful," the golfer said. "But Jacksonville fans have been fantastic to me, so I'm hoping someone is beating him up right now."

MUM'S THE WORD

rishman Padraig Harrington was uncharacteristically hitting some bad shots into the gallery at the 2006 BMW Championship in Wentworth, England. In fact, he hit his mother, Breda, with an errant tee shot. Fortunately, she wasn't hurt.

Later in the round, he smacked another wayward drive that nearly struck her again. He hurried over to check on Breda, but rather than tell her to duck for cover next time, he told her, "Maybe you should start standing behind the green—right in line with the pin."

BLUNT ANSWER

The 1991 Ryder Cup—dubbed the War by the Shore—was a nerve-racking competition at Kiawah Island, South Carolina, where the Americans were desperate to reclaim the trophy that the Europeans had held since 1985.

Late on the final day, the Americans were holding onto a 1-point lead when Hale Irwin battled Europe's Bernhard Langer. The pressure built as the two reached the Ocean Course's seaside 197-yard, par-3 17th hole. Irwin, who was up by one stroke, could hardly breathe from the tension and missed the green with his tee shot.

Walking toward the green, he noticed European player Seve Ballesteros in the gallery talking to a teammate in Spanish. Trying to keep things light, Irwin asked, "Hey, Seve, what did you say to him?"

The fiery Ballesteros, who had been accused of gamesmanship throughout the event, looked Irwin squarely in the eyes and told him, "I said, 'Too bad you didn't knock it in the water.'"

STRIKING A HIGH NOTE

On his way to winning the Nationwide Tour's Cox Classic in 2005 at Champions Run Country Club in Omaha, Jason Gore struck a horrible shot that smacked into the groin of a guy in the gallery.

Gore went over to the fan and apologized. Then the golfer took out a new ball, signed it "Sorry," and handed it to the spectator. "Are you sure you're okay?" Gore asked.

"Yeah," said the fan, "but I'll be singing soprano for a while."

WHAT'S GOOD FOR THE GOOSE

During a practice round at a pro-am, LPGA veteran Rosie Jones and her playing partners were standing at a tee that butted up to the backyard of one of the swank homes that lined the course. She caught a glimpse of several roofers toiling on a gable of the home.

The women were chuckling rather loudly over a joke but they stopped when they heard one of the roofers yell, "Quiet please! Can't you see we're trying to work up here?"

LOVE–HATE RELATIONSHIP

A t the AT&T Pebble Beach National Pro–Am, comedian Ray Romano hit back-to-back bad shots, prompting one fan in the gallery to shout good-naturedly, "Hey, Ray, why bother to play?"

Not skipping a beat, Romano replied, "I play golf because I need more reasons to hate myself. When you do a show called *Everybody Loves Raymond,* you need to balance it out."

HIGH AND DRY

Ian Woosnam couldn't believe his luck when he saw his ball had landed in a spectator's discarded beer cup after an errant shot at the 2004 WGC-EMC World Cup at Kiawah Island's Ocean Course.

The shot left the diminutive Woosie, the 1991 Masters champion, craving a refreshing chug of suds. When the Welshman went up to his ball, an official gave him relief. The golfer plucked the ball out of the cup and in a mocking groan said to the gallery, "There's no beer left."

ADMITTING HIS SHORTCOMINGS

As he stepped off the course at a country club in New York, Horton Smith, the tall, handsome Masters winner in 1934 and 1936, was offered a cigarette by an attractive woman. He refused.

The woman asked, "Don't you drink, either?"

Smith shook his head.

"No vices, honey?" she asked.

"Sure, I have," replied Smith. "I'm often short on my long putts."

IT'S QUANTITY, NOT QUALITY, THAT COUNTS

Lloyd Mangrum had a short putt for par on the 9th hole at Red Run Golf Club in the 1948 Motor City Open. His ball just barely reached the front of the cup and then dropped in after hanging a fraction of a second.

A woman in the gallery shouted, "That wasn't a very good stroke, Mr. Mangrum."

Replied the golfer, "Lady, are we playing *how* or *how many*?"

UP CLOSE AND PERSONAL

Arizona Senator Barry Goldwater enjoyed playing golf even though he wasn't that good off the tee.

At the 1965 Phoenix Open Pro-Am, Goldwater slammed a wicked wayward drive that veered thirty yards into the gallery, glancing off the forehead of a male spectator, who was not seriously injured. At the end of the round, Goldwater, the Republican presidential contender who lost the 1964 election, was asked by reporters how he felt about beaning a fan with his errant tee shot.

Growled Goldwater, "I'll take responsibility for hitting the ball. But he needs to take responsibility too."

"And why is that?" asked a reporter.

Replied the senator, "He was standing too close to my ball."

NOT LOOKING HIS AGE

In 1951, a year after winning the first of his three British Open titles, South African Bobby Locke was blistering the course at the St. Paul Open on his way to winning by a record 19 strokes. After hitting his drive on the final hole, Locke was walking to his ball while acknowledging the cheers from the huge gallery.

As the caddie handed him his club, Locke overheard a nearby spectator tell the person next to him, "This old guy from Africa sure is good."

Locke, who was thirty-four at the time, turned to the fan and asked, "How old do you think I am?"

The spectator answered, "About forty-five."

Locke shook his head and said, "Well, you are eleven years off."

Replied the fan, "Good god, don't tell me you're fifty-six!"

IT'S ALL RELATIVE

Lee Trevino was battling Bob Charles for the lead in the final round of the 1991 GTE Suncoast Classic in Florida. But then Trevino blew up on the 17th hole with a triple bogey 8.

As he trudged to the last tee, Trevino heard someone in the gallery say to another spectator, "Can you believe it? Trevino got an 8."

Half smiling, half sneering, Trevino said, "Yeah, well, it's a hell of a lot better than a nine."

DAMN THOSE PLANTS

Ky Laffoon, a touring pro in the 1930s and 1940s, seldom could make it through a tournament without exploding in anger. The intensity of his tirades embarrassed his wife, Irene, who in 1939 threatened to leave him if he didn't curb his volatile temper.

"I promise golf won't trigger a temper tantrum," he swore to her.

True to his word, Laffoon seemed like a new man at the next tournament. He was totally in control of his emotions through the first two rounds. But then trouble brewed on the 15th hole in the next round when his drive landed deep in a bed of honeysuckle. His face grew red, but he refrained from making a scene.

He found his ball, but after three futile swings, Laffoon let loose like a burst dam, unleashing a torrent of swear words that had spectators blushing as far away as the clubhouse. That's precisely where Irene, whose hands were over her ears, was headed.

Laffoon raced after her, and when he caught up with her, he pleaded, "Don't leave me, sweetheart. I wasn't cussing about golf. I just hate honeysuckle."

FOLLOWING HER SUGGESTION

Clayton Heafner, a hotheaded pro in the 1940s and 1950s, was having a tough time in a tournament near his hometown of Charlotte, North Carolina. In the second round, he couldn't find the fairways with a map and compass.

After sending yet another shot into the rough, he decided he'd had enough. He ordered his caddie, "Pick up my ball. We're through."

From out of the gallery, a petite older woman stepped forward and admonished Heafner. "You can't just quit in a tournament. Where's your sportsmanship? Where's your duty to try your best? You shouldn't pick up your ball."

Heafner squinted at her and nodded. "You're absolutely right, ma'am," he said sweetly. Then, turning to his caddie, he growled. "Don't pick it up." As Heafner strode off to the clubhouse, he shouted, "Just leave the goddamn thing there!"

TWO-TIMER

Golf fan Chuck MacDonald was in the gallery enjoying the action at the 1996 U.S. Open at Oakland Hills Country Club in Bloomfield, Michigan.

The fifty-one-year-old spectator was sitting near the 16th green when Steve Lowery pulled his approach shot. The ball took a hop off a slope and struck MacDonald on the head. Although dazed, the fan was not seriously hurt and declined any medical attention.

He chose to stay because, he thought, what are the odds of getting hit again?

Apparently, they were pretty darn good because a few hours later, Payne Stewart sent a nasty hook from the fairway that slammed into MacDonald's head. This time, the spectator suffered a large bloody gash that required treatment.

Needless to say, he got the hint and left the course. "I don't think I'm coming back here anymore," he muttered to members of the gallery.

NATURE'S CALL

During the 1960 World Series of Golf at Firestone Country Club in Akron, Ohio, Jim Ferree's second shot on the 4th hole bounced off the green, rolled past the spectators, and landed near two outdoor privies, one of which was occupied.

Just before Ferree was set to hit his next shot, an official pushed his way through the gallery and said loudly, "Wait, Jim. There's a man in the outhouse. He's liable to open the door just when you hit."

The crowd turned and stared at the privy door, waiting for it to open. But at that point, the outhouse occupant had no intention of making a grand exit. Instead, everyone heard a muffled voice from inside shout, "Go ahead! Hit!"

ACE LOW

During a practice round at Carnoustie in Scotland the week before the 1975 British Open, Tom Weiskopf nailed a wind-battered hole in one on the 8th hole. But he was miffed when his ace drew very little reaction from the Scottish gallery.

The puzzled pro approached a pair of elderly locals and asked, "Didn't you see my drive go in the hole?"

"Aye, laddie, we did," said one of them.

"You saw it, yet you didn't even clap," Weiskopf complained.

The second Scot countered, "Boot laddie, it didn't coont now, did it?"

A GOOD FAN DEFINED

The *Charlotte* (North Carolina) *Observer* held a contest, challenging readers to define a good spectator at the Kemper Open. The winning entry was sent in by Judith Dunkle of Charlotte: "A perfect spectator must have the eye of an eagle, the neck of a giraffe, the skin of an alligator, and the bladder of an elephant."

ONE WAY TO SILENCE A HECKLER

When Canadian golfer Moe Norman was on his game, no one was more accurate as a shot maker. But there were times when his putter betrayed him. At the 1971 Quebec Open, he held a one-stroke lead coming to the final hole, but he four-putted to finish second.

The next week he was playing a practice round before the Canadian Open. As Norman approached the tee of a 233-yard, par-3 hole, a spectator needled him by asking, "Any four-putts today?"

Norman teed up a ball in silence and hit it straight at the pin. He watched the ball's flight a moment, then turned to the fan and said, "Not putting today." The ball landed on the front of the green and rolled into the cup for an ace.

BELLY-WHOPPER

Donna Horton-White, who competed on the LPGA Tour from 1977 to 1992, played when she was pregnant.

One time during a tournament when she was in her seventh month of pregnancy, she holed a twisting twenty-five-foot putt. The fans gave her a rousing ovation. As she walked off the green, she patted her belly and told the gallery, "That putt was so good I could hear the baby applaud."

PRESS CARDS

NEW-FOUND FAME

By making three birdies in a four-hole stretch on the back nine of the final round, in cold, windy conditions, Zach Johnson won the 2007 Masters, his first major.

His surprising victory brought the unknown champion the coveted green jacket and more than $1.3 million. It also meant an invitation to appear the next evening on *The Late Show with David Letterman*.

In honor of his triumph, the modest Iowan was asked to deliver Dave's nightly Top 10 list. In a perfect deadpan delivery, Johnson recited the "Top Ten Things I Can Say Now That I've Won the Masters." Among them:

- "I'm going to spend the prize money on Mountain Dew and beef jerky."
- "It's a magical week: First I win the Masters, and now I get to tell lame jokes on a third-rate talk show."
- "Thanks to global warming, next year I'm playing without pants."

And, finally, there was this: "Even I've never heard of me."

RIGHT ON!

During a 2004 tournament, CBS golf analyst Peter Kostis watched one of Tiger Woods's drives flare far off the mark.

Referring to Michael Moore's Oscar-winning anti-war documentary *Fahrenheit 9/11,* Kostis told his television audience, "This is so far right that Michael Moore is going to do a documentary on it."

IRONING OUT
THE DIFFERENCES

Golf announcer Judy Rankin is a keen observer of the trends on the PGA and LPGA tours. She noticed the difference between the way the men and women golfers wear their clothes on the course: "I swear, if you had an ironing contest between the PGA Tour and the LPGA Tour, right now the men would win."

GREAT PERKS

After Todd Hamilton stunned the golf world by winning the 2004 British Open, he appeared on David Letterman's show, where the then little-known golfer read "The Top 10 Perks of Winning the British Open."

Among them:

- "Everywhere I go I'm recognized by middle-aged fat guys."
- "Get to appear on MTV's *Pimp My Cart*."
- "Claret Jug is full of sambuca."
- "You become a household name like past winners David Brown and George Duncan."

- "For the next week only, Big Ben will be renamed 'Big Todd.'"

And the number one perk for winning the British Open? "I've been filling some divots, if you know what I mean."

GROWN-UP BLOOPER

Moments after Davis Love III won the 2003 AT&T Pebble Beach National Pro-Am, CBS-TV sportscaster Jim Nantz was in the tower over the 18th green talking to film legend Clint Eastwood live on the air.

Nantz told him that Davis's late father had been a huge Eastwood fan. "I'll bet you didn't know that when Davis was a young boy, one of the first adult films his father ever took him to see was one of yours," Nantz said.

Eastwood gave him a sly grin and said, "Why, Jim, I have never made an adult film in my life."

WHAT A PISSER

While getting miked up for TV host Peter Kessler's live show on the Golf Channel, Dave Hill, a thirteen-time winner on the PGA Tour in the 1960s and 1970s, told him, "I might have to use the men's room during the show because I have a little problem."

"You can't go to the bathroom during the show," Kessler warned. "It's ten to eight so unload your bladder now, because you have to sit here for an hour. This is live television."

Hill didn't have to go at that moment. But at 8:30, after telling Kessler during each of three previous commercial breaks that he needed the bathroom, Hill announced, "I'm going." One of the audio technicians unhooked the wires, and Hill bolted.

Meanwhile, the show's producer ran a long series of commercials. Even so, when Kessler came back on the air, he was still alone. So he pretended that Hill was seated across from him as the camera came in tight on him. Kessler then asked a question that went on and on and on.

By now, Hill had returned and, while still off-camera, was miked again. The camera then went to Hill so fast that the audio technician had to crouch behind Hill's chair because there wasn't time to run off the set.

Finally Kessler wrapped up the relentlessly long question and waited for a response. Having just settled in, Hill looked blankly at the host and said, "Could you repeat that?"

WRITER'S CRAMP

Famous writer Dan Jenkins has poked fun at golfers for years with his hilarious barbs that sometimes cut too deep for the thin skinned.

Jenkins once wrote, "What fun is it to be Johnny Miller if the highlight of your social life is watching your kids turn over glasses of milk in a Marriott?"

After George Archer won the 1969 Masters, Jenkins wrote that the golfer still wouldn't have any charisma if he rode in a golf cart with Jill St. John, a sexy young actress at the time. A few days later, the writer received a note from Archer's wife that said, "I'll have you know that my husband has more charisma than Joe Namath and Gary Cooper combined." Jenkins thought about writing her back, saying something like, "I agree with you, inasmuch as Joe Namath is now crippled and Gary Cooper is dead." But he didn't.

At the 1975 U.S. Open at the Medinah Country Club, Lou Graham had just beaten John Mahaffey in a playoff. In the hot, humid press tent, Jenkins was clacking away on his portable typewriter, trying to beat a deadline when someone tapped him on the shoulder. It was Graham's wife, Patsy. She smiled at Jenkins and said, "Be nice, Dan. He's really a good guy."

There were no barbs in Jenkins's dispatch.

NOT ADDING UP

After Tiger Woods went winless in the majors in 2003, the press began wondering whether he had lost his edge. The speculation prompted *Denver Post* columnist Jim Armstrong to write, "If my math is right, Tiger has three mansions, a couple of seven-car garages and a blond swimsuit model for a girlfriend. Yep, he's in a slump all right."

WATCHING TV CAN BE BAD FOR YOU

Kirk Nelson, a forty-three-year-old Hawaiian club pro, got a taste of life in the spotlight during the first round of the 2003 Sony Open when he hit a 256-yard 3-wood second shot to the 18th green.

The shot was so well struck, TV producers decided to show it on the giant screen behind the green for all, including Nelson, to see.

For Nelson, however, the glory was short lived. "I got so excited watching the replay," he confessed later to reporters, "that I three-putted for par."

NO GIMMES

While playing golf with President Gerald Ford one day, hockey great Gordie Howe wanted to concede Ford's simple two-foot putt. The president sportingly insisted on putting—and then missed. "We won't count that one," Howe said. Ford shook his head. Pointing to the reporters crowding around the green, the president said, "Maybe you won't count it, but they certainly will."

HE FINALLY GOT HIS WISH

Jack Nicklaus played his worst round ever in his professional career when he carded a woeful 83 at the 1981 British Open at Royal St. George's in England. When he came off the 18th green, he told reporters, "I'll talk about today tomorrow."

For Nicklaus to shoot an 83 was bigger news than a Tour rookie shooting a 63. Across the Atlantic, news commentator Paul Harvey told his radio audience, "All my life I wanted to play like Jack Nicklaus, and now I do."

STILL A SWINGER

Roger Maltbie was part of the NBC team covering the 1999 U.S. Open at Pinehurst (which was won by Payne Stewart). After the first round, Maltbie and announcer Dan Hicks were in the tower at 18 and decided to do an interview with Sam Snead, who had recently turned eighty-seven.

The producers were advised that Snead had good days and bad days, so they decided to tape the interview because they didn't want to embarrass the golfing legend in case this was one of his bad days.

The interview with Maltbie and Hicks started slowly for Snead, who seemed a little disjointed and confused. But then he recalled his disaster at the 1939 U.S. Open when he bogeyed and triple-bogeyed the last two holes. "You know," he told Hicks, "I sat down and thought about it once, and if

I had shot 69 in the final round of the Open, I'd have won eight of them."

From that moment on, Snead was lucid and spoke clearly. At one point, Hicks asked him, "What's the secret of a long, healthy life?"

"Well, I never drank much," Snead replied. "Always took pretty good care of myself. Got to bed early, got a lot of sleep." Then, grinning and winking at Hicks, he added, "Of course, I did shake those bedsprings every now and then."

SOUNDS OF SILENCE

When Jim Nantz, the voice of the Masters on CBS-TV, was reporting his first tournament at Augusta National in 1986, he learned that the hole placement on the par-3 16th would be on the back-left of the green for the final round.

During the preproduction meeting with Frank Chirkinian, who was the producer of the golf telecast, the twenty-six-year-old Nantz asked, "What should I say if somebody makes a hole in one?"

"Son," said the veteran TV man, "I'll tell you exactly what to say if somebody makes a hole in one at 16: nothing!

This is a visual medium, you idiot! Now, get out of my office and get down there to rehearsal!"

CHOOSING HIS OWN COURSE

On his way to winning the 1979 British Open at Royal Lytham, twenty-two-year-old Spaniard Seve Ballesteros seemed to play golf everywhere but on the fairway. In four days of competition, he managed to keep his tee shot on the fairway only nine times. He also was in the bunker fifteen times and saved par fourteen times.

Ballesteros's swashbuckling, scrambling style inspired Colin Maclaine, chair of the championship committee, to write, "He chose not to use the course, but preferred his own, which mainly consisted of hay fields, car parks, grandstands, drop zones and even ladies' clothing."

THE DANGERS OF GOLF (CIRCA 1922)

During Prohibition, at least one official report called golf as dangerous as bootleg gin. In the report, written in 1922, the federal director of prohibition

BRING BACK GARY MCCORD

While covering the 17th hole at the 1994 Masters, witty CBS golf reporter Gary McCord told the world that the green was so fast it seemed to be bikini waxed. Then he described the difficulty of recovering from overly long approach shots by saying there were body bags buried behind the green.

The folks at Augusta National, notoriously sensitive about how their beloved course is described, were not amused and banned McCord from ever again announcing at the Masters.

Champions Tour golfer Peter Jacobsen, who's known for his own sharp wit, believed that McCord had suffered enough, so in 2003 Jacobsen wrote this song about returning his pal to the Masters telecasts:

"I want to hear Gary McCord/Whenever he's on I'm never bored/I like Gary McCord/Masters officials, we're begging you please/We wish you wouldn't take yourselves so seriously/Bring back Gary McCord/We want him back/Let's send him a fax/No more bikini wax/Or body bags/This whole thing's been such a drag."

enforcement for Minnesota gave these four reasons why golf was bad for family men:

"First, golf is not intended for anybody under 55 years of age.

"Second, it encourages idleness and shiftlessness.

"Third, men neglect their families and their business duties to play the game.

"And fourth, young men are tempted to take on expenses they cannot meet and so frequently are led to commit crimes."

WELL, HUSH MY MOUTH

After fourteen Tour victories including the 1964 U.S. Open, Ken Venturi became a color commentator for CBS Sports.

He was taping some golf tips for a 1980 telecast, which included demonstrating a wedge shot. After hitting a few practice balls, Venturi told the cameraman to start shooting. "The wedge shot from seventy yards requires a lot of knee action and a smooth stroke," Venturi said to the camera. "And if this shot is hit correctly, the ball should take three bounces, jump left, and go into the hole." Venturi took a swing and, to his amazement, saw the ball take three bounces, jump to the left, and fall into the hole. The cameraman was so excited he shouted, "He sank the S.O.B.!"

TWO FOR WON

The 1954 U.S. Open at Baltusrol's Lower Course—the first Open to be nationally televised—featured a star-studded field that included Ben Hogan, Sam Snead, Cary Middlecoff, and Jimmy Demaret. But in a surprise, the winner was journeyman pro Ed Furgol, who had overcome a childhood playground accident that had disfigured his arm.

Furgol, who held a one-stroke lead going into the final hole, needed a par to win the title. But he badly hooked his tee shot into the trees that separated the Lower Course from the Upper Course. He played his second shot onto a fairway on the Upper Course, then knocked his approach onto the Lower Course's 18th green. He tapped it in for a par to beat Gene Littler by a shot.

The way Furgol played the hole astounded veteran golf reporter Red Hoffman, who wrote, "First time I've ever seen a guy win a major by playing two courses on one hole."

PERISH THE THOUGHT

At the 1986 Masters, Jack Nicklaus was making a charge that ultimately earned him his sixth green jacket.

When Nicklaus reached the 16th tee, sports reporter Jim Nantz, who was covering the hole during the CBS telecast, was describing how historic it would be if the Bear won again at Augusta.

One of the CBS rules for the on-air talent was never to talk over a shot. So Nantz hushed up as Nicklaus stood over his tee shot. But then the golfer backed off. Knowing that he had another thirty seconds to kill before Nicklaus would hit his drive, Nantz was completely out of material and turned to his colleague, analyst Tom Weiskopf.

"Tom Weiskopf, what is going through Jack's mind right now?" Nantz asked on the air. "He has not experienced this kind of a streak in a long time."

With sarcasm dripping from his voice, Weiskopf told Nantz and a nationwide audience, "If I knew the way he thought, I would've won this tournament."

BUILDING SUSPENSE

Despite his love for golf, Jack Lemmon just wasn't that good at it.

During the telecast of the 1969 Bing Crosby National Pro-Am, broadcaster Jim McKay of ABC got off this classic line: "And now here's Jack Lemmon about to hit that all-important eighth shot."

CURSES TO THOSE COURSES

Sometimes a typographical error can be more accurate than the correct word.

In 1965, the state of North Carolina published a tourism booklet that promoted golf. In it was this sentence: "Famous midsouth resorts include Pinehurst and Southern Pines, where it is said that there are more golf curses per square mile than anywhere else in the world."

Then again, maybe this wasn't a typo after all.

FUN AND GAMES

Aaccording to a 1988 survey conducted by advice columnist Ann Landers, when golfers were asked to choose between sex and their favorite sport, the pleasures of the flesh came in second.

One golfer wrote Landers, "While playing golf, your partners give you praise and encouragement even when you are not performing well. I don't remember this ever happening in the bedroom."

SLIP OF THE TONGUE

Jimmy Demaret was an announcer for ABC on the first nationally televised golfing event: the 1953 World Championship of Golf.

In an exciting conclusion at the Tam O'Shanter Country Club in Chicago, Lew Worsham, the year's leading money winner and 1947 U.S. Open champion, sank a dramatic 104-yard wedge shot on the final hole for an eagle that won the prestigious event.

When the ball was hit, Demaret informed his broadcast audience, "He's hit it fat. It will probably be short. It just hit the front edge of the green. It's got no chance. It's rolling, but it will stop. It's rolling toward the cup. Well, I'll be goddamned! He sank it!"

WHAT'S REALLY IMPORTANT

The following newspaper ad appeared in the *Midland* (Texas) *Reporter–Telegram* in 1993:

LOST: GOLFING HUSBAND AND DOG

LAST SEEN AT RATLIFF RANCH GOLF LINKS

REWARD FOR DOG

IMPOSSIBLE TO FORGET

Raymond Floyd handily won the 1976 Masters by eight strokes over Ben Crenshaw and eleven over Jack Nicklaus and Larry Ziegler.

During the final round, CBS golf analyst Ken Venturi was asked whether anyone could overcome Floyd's commanding lead.

"Yes," he said. "It's very conceivable. I know someone who lost an eight-shot lead. Matter of fact, I saw him in the mirror this morning."

(As an amateur in 1956, Venturi took the first-round lead at the Masters and was up by four shots going into Sunday. But then he three-putted six times and shot 80, winding up as runner-up by one stroke to Jack Burke Jr.)

HOW QUICKLY THEY TURN ON YOU

American-born Australian Aaron Baddeley gave up a sensational amateur career to turn pro in 2000. At first, the down-under newspapers praised the nineteen-year-old. But he never could get untracked in his rookie year. After shooting lackluster rounds of 80 and 75 at the 2000 Memorial Tournament, the rattled teen had to contend with some hurtful Aussie headlines. The one that made him flinch the most: "From Baddeley to Worse."

IF ONLY BROADCASTERS COULD TAKE MULLIGANS

Australian Ian Baker-Finch, best known for winning the 1991 British Open, became a TV golf analyst. One time he was covering the Australian Open when the cameras zoomed in on a school of fish in a lake on the course. At that moment, he said something that he wished he could have taken back. He told the TV viewers, "You know, those fish are pretty big. They've been nibbling on the members' balls for years."

THIS JUST IN

Overcome with joy after winning the 2006 BMW Asian Open, Gonzalo Fernandez-Castaño gushed on live TV, "I'm so happy about this I think I'm going to get married!" Realizing his comments might reach his girlfriend, Alicia, who wasn't there, he backtracked. "But I haven't asked her yet, so don't say anything."

Too late. But he made it official the next day, and the couple wed several months after the victory.

STRONG ADVICE

When he was a guest on *The Tonight Show* in 1965, Jimmy Demaret was asked by host Johnny Carson, "Will you please analyze my swing?"

"Of course," said Demaret.

After showing off his stroke, Carson asked the golfer, "So, what do you think of my golf swing?"

Answered Demaret, "If I were you, I'd lay off for a couple of weeks—and then quit."

NAME DROPPER

Lloyd Braun was the attorney for Larry David when David was head writer and executive producer of the hit TV show *Seinfeld*. The two also are golfing buddies.

Friends of David know that one of the real challenges when taking him golfing is that occasionally, if he's not playing well, he wants to quit. So it has become a running joke among his playing partners, "Are we going to get him through all eighteen holes?"

One day in 1995, Braun was having a great game while David was playing horribly. By the back nine, David wanted to quit, but Braun didn't want to finish the round alone, so he kept trying to think of ways to make David stay. After the 16th hole, David was starting to walk off the course.

"Wait," said Braun. "Why don't we have a bet for the last two holes?"

"Okay, what are the stakes?"

"If you win, you can use my name any way you please in a *Seinfeld* episode."

"You're on—if you give me a shot a hole."

They shook on it. Motivated by the wager or blessed with luck, David tied Braun on the 17th and won the final hole after the attorney shanked his drive out of bounds.

Braun didn't think anything more about the bet, figuring David would forget about it. Five months later, the attorney was sitting in his office when David called him. "So, uh, Laurie [David's wife] says I had to call you because I'm using your name in the show."

"When are you taping it?"

"In an hour."

"Why are you telling me now, Larry?"

"Well, Laurie says that, you know, if you want it out, I should take it out."

"How many times is my name used in the show?"

"A few times."

"What's 'a few times'?"

"Uhhh, maybe about eighty."

In the episode, Lloyd Braun is a former childhood neighbor of George Costanza and grew up to become a handsome, politically connected businessman—and also a former patient in a mental hospital. George's clueless mother wishes her son would emulate Lloyd Braun. A subtle running gag in the episode was that the character always was referred to as Lloyd Braun, not just Lloyd or Braun.

In one scene, Braun is working at a computer store for George's dad, Frank.

George: What is Lloyd Braun doing here?

Frank: Your mother recommended him.

George: Yeah, of course she did. That's all I ever heard growing up is, 'Why can't you be more like Lloyd Braun?' Did you know he was in a mental institution?

Frank: I didn't read his résumé.

A MATTER of COURSE

SWEET FEAT

The notorious "Donut Bunker" is a circular sand trap in the middle of the 6th green at Riviera Country Club in Pacific Palisades, California, site of the Nissan Open.

It was at that 199-yard, par-3 hole in the 2004 tournament that Kevin Sutherland landed his ball in the Donut for what looked like the makings of an unfortunate bogey or worse.

But Sutherland amazed the gallery and caddie John Wood when he holed his shot from the Donut for a most unusual par. As the two walked off the green, Wood told the golfer, "I'll bet that's the first time a guy hit a green in regulation and had a sand save on the same hole."

CHOOSE YOUR DEATH

Mike Reid surprised lots of his golfing colleagues before the first round of the 1998 U.S. Open when he said he loved the rough at the Olympic Club in San Francisco, adding that he wished they played a course like that "every two months."

His frustrations rose in concert with his scores and by Sunday, after he had finished at 16-over 296, he had changed his tune. "If we played courses like this regularly," Reid said, "the only decision would be razor blades or gas."

PROVING HIS POINT

In 1948 the board of directors of the Baltusrol Golf Club in Springfield, New Jersey, wanted to improve its two courses so it would be considered a venue for a future U.S. Open. Robert Trent Jones, the best golf course designer of his era, was hired to make the necessary changes.

To the ire of the touring pros, Jones believed in tough courses that featured huge bunkers, ponds, creeks, and undulating greens to counteract the improving equipment. "The shattering of par without a proper challenge is a fraud," he often said. "I make them [golfers] play par."

If the PGA Tour players designed courses, Jones once said, "You would have dead flat greens and dead flat fairways, very little rough and very few traps. That kind of course wouldn't require an architect. You could order it from a Sears Roebuck catalog."

For one of the alterations he made at Baltusrol's Lower Course, Jones shoved back the tee on the 194-yard, par-3 4th hole, which plays over water. But members complained that he had made the hole too difficult and that it wouldn't be fair to the pros who would play there for the 1954 U.S. Open.

Jones was determined to end the squawking. At his suggestion, he, club pro Johnny Farrell, and two board members headed to the 4th tee to play the hole while other club members watched. Hitting from the 165-yard members' tee, Farrell and the two members each lofted balls that carried the pond, cleared the stone retaining wall, and landed on the green.

Then Jones stepped up and swung his 4-iron. His ball sailed over the water, plopped onto the green, and rolled six feet straight into the cup for a hole in one.

Turning to the stunned onlookers, Jones declared, "Gentlemen, the hole is fair. Eminently fair."

TEE(JUANA) TIME

Joe Kirkwood, an Australian-born trick shot artist and tournament player who won three PGA events in 1923, was one of Walter Hagen's best friends. Occasionally they took time out to appear in golfing exhibitions throughout the world.

In 1928 the pair played at Caliente Golf Course in Tijuana, Mexico, where the fairways were nothing more than parched, arid ground. Afterwards, in the locker room, Kirkwood told Hagen, "It was like playing in a desert out there, with the dry heat and all that dust. Next time I'll bring a camel."

"You're just spoiled," kidded Hagen. "You just want to play on wide, manicured fairways and big smooth greens."

"I can play on any course," countered Kirkwood.

"Oh, yeah? Tell you what. How about we make our own course and play on it?" said Hagen.

"What do you mean?" asked Kirkwood.

"Let's use the streets of Tijuana," Hagen said. "We'll play from the locker room back to our hotel room. The first one who gets back and knocks the ball into the toilet bowl wins."

"You're on," Kirkwood said. "For how much?"

"Let's keep it friendly," said Hagen. "Fifty bucks."

Each with a caddie by his side, the golfers set out from the clubhouse on the mile-long "course" to their hotel. As a growing crowd of Mexicans clustered around them making side bets, Hagen and Kirkwood banged their shots down the dusty driveway of the golf club and onto the main street.

Followed by a cheering gallery in sombreros and sandals, the pair played through the center of town. The zany twosome drove their golf balls past giggling, barefoot, tortilla-making muchachas and through an open-air fruit market of startled merchants. All the while, Hagen and Kirkwood dodged trucks, buses, and donkey carts and more often than not brought traffic to a screeching halt.

Hagen arrived at the hotel grounds first, ahead of Kirkwood by a few minutes. The Haig lofted a shot that carried the flowerbeds. Then he belted his ball into the lobby and played it up the stairs, down the corridor, and finally into their room.

But infuriatingly, Hagen failed to knock his ball into the toilet bowl because he couldn't get his wedge to pick it off the floor. After a dozen unsuccessful attempts, he saw Kirkwood enter the bathroom. "Move over," said the trick shot artist. Then, with one deft swing of his pitching wedge, Kirkwood plopped his ball into the toilet, declaring, "Now that's what I call a fifty-dollar splash."

HIGH SIGNS

During a practice round before the 1926 U.S. Open at Scioto Country Club in Columbus, Ohio, Scottish-born pro Jock Hutchinson, winner of the 1920 PGA Championship and 1921 British Open, complained to an official about the tall grass.

"I lost a ball in your rough today," Hutchinson told him. "I dropped another ball over my shoulder and lost it too. And while I was looking for that one, I lost my caddie."

BETTER THAN A GOLF CART

One of Willie Nelson's favorite golf partners is Darrell Royal, the former University of Texas football coach.

During one round at the singer's Pedernales Golf Club in Spicewood, Texas, Royal asked Nelson, "I heard you sometimes play this course in the winter in your Mercedes. Is that really true?"

"Yep," said the golf-addicted country and western star.

"Why the Mercedes?" asked the coach.

"Because it's got the best heater."

TOO TOUGH FOR MERE MORTALS

Scotsman Jack McLean and Atlanta-bred Charlie Yates played against each other during the 1936 Walker Cup matches at New Jersey's difficult Pine Valley Golf Club.

Although on opposite teams, the two competitors shared the same feelings about the course. After the American amateurs trounced the British amateurs, McLean and Yates collaborated on the following ode:

> We think that we shall never see
> A tougher course than Pine Valley.
> Trees and traps wherever we go,
> And clumps of earth flying through the air.
> This course made for you and me,
> But only God can make a three.

OF COURSE IT'S A COARSE COURSE

Some of the rules at Willie Nelson's Pedernales Golf Club:

- When another player is shooting, no player should talk, whistle, hum, clink coins, or pass gas.
- Excessive displays of affection are discouraged. Violators must replace divots and will be penalized five strokes.
- Replace divots, smooth footprints in bunkers, brush backtrail with branches, park car under brush, and have the office tell your spouse you're in a conference.
- No more than twelve in your foursome.
- Gambling is forbidden, of course, unless you're stuck or you need a legal deduction for charitable or educational expenses.
- No bikinis, mini-skirts, skimpy see-through, or sexually exploitative attire allowed. Except on women.

What is par for the course? According to Nelson, "Par is whatever I say it is. I've got one hole that's a par-23, and yesterday I damn-near birdied the sucker!"

TOPLESS GOLFERS

Irrepressible funnymen George Burns and Harpo Marx were playing at the swank Hillcrest Country Club on a sweltering summer day in Los Angeles. During their round, they doffed their shirts, unaware that this was against club rules.

Quicker than a drive down the fairway, an offended club member known for his snobbery complained to the caddie master. He, in turn, rushed into the clubhouse to report this grievous breach of club etiquette to the haughty Greens Committee.

The committee chair dashed out to the course and caught up with the bare-chested pair. Waving the sacred Hillcrest book of regulations under the noses of the twosome, the snooty chairman announced, "You can't play like that. It clearly states in our book of regulations that shirts must be worn by members at all times."

"But we can appear on a public beach without tops," Burns argued. "Why must we wear them here?"

"Sorry," said the chairman. "No shirts, no play."

Marx and Burns read through the list of rules carefully and saw that they indeed could not go topless, so they reluctantly donned their shirts.

"We're sorry," said Burns. "It's only right that we follow the rules."

"I'm glad you see it that way." Having dealt with the day's most serious offense, the smug chair returned triumphantly to the clubhouse.

Back on the course, the pair agreed that whatever behavior wasn't spelled out in the club rules could not be considered a rule and therefore was perfectly permissible.

Five minutes later, the caddie master burst into the clubhouse with news even more disturbing than before. "Come quick!" he shouted to the chairman. "Now those actors are out there playing without pants!"

THROUGH
THE GRACE OF GOD

San Francisco amateur Matt Palacio has proven to many golfers that Pebble Beach is indeed blessed with divine providence.

He was playing in the 1965 Bing Crosby National Pro-Am when he smacked a wayward drive on the seaside 18th. As he watched his ball sail in the general direction of Japan, Palacio muttered, "Only God can save that one."

Just then the waves receded. The ball struck a bare rock and miraculously caromed back onto a favorable spot on the fairway. Palacio gazed up to the heavens and shouted, "Thank you, God!"

SCOTTISH FORE!CASTS

Bad weather is considered par for the course when you play any of the links in the British Isles. All you need to do is dress appropriately, says Nick Price, winner of the 1994 British Open and PGA Championship.

According to Price, a general rule for British Open players is to decipher the weather reports of a Scotsman. "If he says, 'It's a wee bit breezy,' it's a 30-mph wind. 'A stiff breeze' means 40 mph. And if he says, 'It might be a chilly mornin',' you'll want to bring your parka and ski gloves."

GONE TO POT

Top pros are so good at escaping from well-manicured bunkers at PGA Tour sites they sometimes aim for the tame traps in order to get a better position for their next shot.

Not at Jack Nicklaus's Memorial Tournament in Columbus, Ohio. It was there that Nicklaus got approval from the PGA to experiment with special rakes that left deep furrows in the sand of the bunkers.

The pros found the results jarring, and Nick Price was heard to lament, "There are pot bunkers and then there are these—they're potluck bunkers."

INSPIRATION FROM ABOVE

Golfers who take golf cart No. 47 at Sea Scape Golf Links along North Carolina's Outer Banks might look up for advice when their golf game starts going down.

If they do, they're not likely to be disappointed. A golfer with a clever sense of humor wrote on the underside of the golf cart roof the following message: "You're looking up. That's your problem."

WACKY FOREIGN COURSE RULES

"You cannot ground your club in addressing the ball, or move anything, however loose or dead it may be."

—Royal Selanger Golf Club, built on an ancient Chinese burial ground near Kuala Lumpur, Malaysia

"If a ball comes to rest within a tail's distance of a sleeping buffalo, it may be removed and dropped no nearer the hole without penalty. More than a tail's length, the ball shall be played as it lies."

—Elephant Hills Country Club, Victoria Falls, Zimbabwe

"If a player's ball hits a running warthog [which runs with its tail pointed straight up], this does not entitle the player to replay the shot, except when the ball strikes the tail, in which case it shall be deemed to have a struck a miniature moving flagpole."

—Elephant Hills Country Club, Victoria Falls, Zimbabwe

"The area known as the Elephant Pit is a water hazard whether or not it contains water."

—Bombay (India) Presidency Golf Club

"If a ball comes to rest in dangerous proximity to a hippo-potamus or crocodile, another ball may be dropped, at a safe distance, no nearer the hole, without penalty."

—Nyanza Club, Kisumu, Kenya

"Ball may be lifted and dropped without penalty . . . from wallaby and bandicoot scrapes, crab holes, stone outcrops, tractor marks and genuine earth cracks."

—Darwin (Australia) Golf Club

"Stones [thrown by herdsmen accompanying cattle grazing on the course] which obstruct a stroke in hazards may be removed free of penalty, and in this case treated as Loose Impediment under Rule 18. . . . A ball lying on any of the footpaths, cutcha roads, cattle and cart tracks, in runnels [watery ruts] adjoining them, in hoof marks or dung on the course, may be lifted and dropped without penalty."

—Bolarum Golf Club, Hyderabad, India

"Dress of intending players shall be supervised by starters. Where shorts are worn, long hose and shoes shall also be worn. No suspenders [garters] are to be showing. If jeans are worn, they are to be worn full length and not rolled."

—Beverly Park Golf Course, Kogarah,
New South Wales, Australia

IN THE CAN

When Becky Lucidi was a rookie on the LPGA Tour in 2007, she wrote in her blog about some of the fascinating names she came across on the outside door of the portable toilets that golfers have used on the course during tournaments.

"It seems hundreds of these blue, brown, green and tan plastic coffins arrive each week at the tournament site," she wrote. "It's sort of a love–hate relationship I have with these odor-ific containers. Normally, not too pleasant to be in for periods longer than, well, however long you can hold your breath, but at the same time, can seem like a couple Tums after a bowl of chili . . . RELIEF."

Here is a ranked list of her favorite names for these toilets:

13. Best Seat in the House
12. Call-a-Head Seating
11. Plop John
10. Royal Flush
 9. Tanks-a-Lot
 8. Wizards of Ooze
 7. UrinBiz.com
 6. Honey Bucket
 5. Blue Castle
 4. The Drop Zone
 3. Oui Oui Enterprises
 2. Willy Make It?
 1. Doody Calls

FAR and AWAY

PAYING ONE WAY
OR THE OTHER

At a fund-raiser for one of her favorite charities, glam golfer Cristie Kerr was asked by a fan how he could play a round with her.

"You could pay to play in an LPGA pro-am and hope you draw me," she replied. "Or you could outbid others vying to play with me in one of my Birdies for Breast Cancer events. The bidding starts at $2,500."

"Are there any other possibilities?" the fan asked.

"Well, there is a much more drastic measure you can take. Shave your legs, take estrogen and work your way up through the Futures Tour. Good luck!"

TIEING ONE ON

At the 2002 Ryder Cup at the De Vere Belfry in Sutton, Coldfield, England, Sam Torrance, the European team's captain, was taking a shower in his hotel room in preparation for a semiformal dinner with both teams and golf dignitaries.

When the phone rang, he jumped out of the shower to answer it. On the line was one of his players, a frantic Pierre Fulke. "Sam, I've got a huge problem," Fulke revealed. "It's the biggest problem of the week. I have to come see you. Right now!"

Torrance's heart began pounding as he wondered what calamity had befallen his player. The captain wrapped a towel around his waist and waited the scant seconds it took Fulke to dash into the room. Fulke's face was ashen.

"Pierre, what in the world is wrong?" Torrance asked.

"Sam, I can't do my tie."

Still dripping from his shower, the relieved captain helped tie Fulke's tie.

SAY "CHEES-EY!"

After fifteen years of taking group pictures of rowdy golfers at Myrtle Beach, Paula Thomas has seen plenty through her viewfinder.

One time, Thomas took a photo of a group of about forty golfers just as one joker raised a bottle of liquor high over his head. It instantly became the focal point of the picture. There were two problems with the photo. One: The guy didn't even belong with the group; he was just a crasher. Two: The golfers were from a Baptist church group.

SIGN OF THE TIMES

During the 2002 PGA Championship at Hazeltine National Golf Club in Chaska, Minnesota, a nearby church decided to turn the event into a lesson for passers-by. Outside the church, the sermon sign read, "Golf is one way God keeps us humble."

ANCIENT, YES, BUT ROYAL?

On his first trip to Scotland, Sam Snead was with fellow pro golfer Lawson Little on a London train bound for the 1946 British Open. Near the end of the journey, Snead spotted what to him looked like a run-down, weedy fairway in the midst of some gray, craggy moors.

The country-bred West Virginian tapped the knee of a proper, well-dressed Scottish gentleman who was sitting across the aisle and said, "Say, that looks like an old, abandoned golf course. What did they call it?"

The blood drained from the Scotsman's face. "My good sir!" he replied haughtily. "That is the Royal and Ancient Club of St. Andrews, founded in 1754. It is where they are playing this year's Open. It is not now, nor ever will be, abandoned!"

"Holy smoke, I'm sorry," said Snead sheepishly. He turned to Little and whispered, "Down home we wouldn't plant cow beets on land like that."

THE SECRET TO WINNING

In 1992, after winning the British Open for the third time, Nick Faldo read in the newspaper that the great Ben Hogan said, "The only modern player I'd give time to is Nick Faldo."

Because Hogan was his hero, Faldo promptly flew to Fort Worth, Texas, for a rare audience with the taciturn Hall of Famer. An intense student of the game and an eager learner, Faldo was hoping to find the secret to winning one of the most prized tournaments in all of golf.

Sitting across the desk from Hogan, Faldo asked, "How do you win the U.S. Open?"

Hogan rested his elbows on his chair's armrest, leaned forward, and replied, "You shoot the lowest score."

After a couple of seconds of silence, Faldo burst out laughing. But Hogan wasn't smiling. "No, seriously," said Faldo, who then repeated the question.

Without batting an eye or cracking a smile, Hogan said, "I'm not kidding. If by Sunday evening you have shot the lowest score, I promise they will give you the medal. I know. I have five of them."

DUAL PERSONALITIES

Famous golf instructor Bob Toski played golf with his good friend Arnold Palmer one day in 1985.

Later, the pair headed to a restaurant. But before they could get in, autograph seekers surrounded Arnie. As always, Palmer patiently signed each piece of paper thrust in front of him. In the midst of his frantic scribbling, Palmer noticed Toski being shoved to the side. Ever the considerate friend, Palmer turned to his fans and said, "Get his autograph too."

A curious young man looked at Toski and asked, "Who are you?"

Without a moment's hesitation, the slightly built golfer deadpanned, "I'm Eddie Arcaro, the famous jockey."

Suddenly, Toski was swamped with autograph requests. He stood there and signed the name of the jockey at least a dozen times as Palmer watched in bemusement. Later, Arnie asked, "Why did you do that?"

"Well," Toski explained, "there I stood with the world's greatest golfer. You didn't think I was going to say I was a golfer too, did you?"

HOW DO YOU SAY "YOU GOT ME" IN SPANISH?

During a tournament in Mexico City years ago, Lee Trevino was on his way to dinner with twenty friends at a fancy restaurant. Riding with him was his good friend Pete Zagganino, a Connecticut lawyer.

Trevino told his pal it was a Mexican custom to express great appreciation to the waiter after the meal was finished. Zagganino, who knew no Spanish, asked Trevino what he should say.

The golfer answered, "Just grab the waiter and say, 'La cuenta, por favor.' And don't worry. I'll let you know when to say it."

After a long and festive meal of drinks, appetizers, more drinks, entrees, more drinks, desserts, and still more drinks, Trevino nudged Zagganino and whispered, "Now, Pete."

Zagganino hailed the waiter and said cheerfully, "La cuenta, por favor." He had no idea that he had just asked the waiter for the bill. As requested, the waiter handed the unsuspecting American a tab for $1,200, while Trevino and his friends bolted from the table.

ELBOW ROOM

eo Diegel, the winner of back-to-back PGA Championships in 1928 and 1929, had a distinct putting style. It was an unorthodox elbows-out technique often called "Diegeling."

He hunched forward over the putt, bent almost 90 degrees at the waist, with both elbows sticking straight out to the side. The forearms formed a straight line, locked by the hands on the putter handle that was parallel to the putting line, with the left elbow pointed at the cup. With his strange putting technique and ball striking ability, Diegel won thirty tournaments.

When he died in 1951, one of his greatest rivals, Walter Hagen, showed up at the funeral with their mutual friend Joe Kirkwood, an Australian pro and trick shot artist. Hagen and Kirkwood waited until the last mourner had left the cemetery. Then the two golfers opened up some beers to toast Diegel, who was buried with his lucky putter.

"We share these beers with you, Leo, for the long trip ahead," the Haig said, holding his bottle high. "May you and your putter rust in peace."

After draining the first of many bottles, Hagen added, "And by the way, how the blazes did they get you in there with those elbows stuck out?"

CHANGING TIMES

Hell-raising rock legend Alice Cooper has long since given up his wild ways and now spends as much time as possible on the golf course, playing at least five times a week to a 3 handicap.

One day the golf nut was backstage talking with another rock legend, the once-volatile Lou Reed. Cooper was surprised to learn that Reed was a recent convert to the sport. "I keep pushing the ball to the right," Reed complained.

"Lighten your right-hand grip so the club will turn over," Cooper advised.

Reed started practicing this motion, totally engrossed in his swing.

Seeing this scene unfold, Cooper told Reed, "Could anyone have dreamed twenty-five years ago, sitting in the Chelsea Hotel, that Lou Reed and Alice Cooper would ever be having this conversation?"

SUCK IT UP

Before the 2007 Bob Hope Chrysler Classic, host George Lopez told reporters that his golf game was momentarily thrown off after he studied a tape of his swing.

"This guy filmed three of my swings, and he was telling me about my spine angle, and I was raising my head, and I wasn't getting the full turn," said the comedian, a 13-handicapper. "Really, after he spoke, the only thing I really looked at when analyzing the tape was whether I looked fat or not.

"I didn't really hear what he had to say. I was figuring out how important it was for me to suck in my stomach. Now I've got to suck it in until Monday."

GOD WORKS IN
MYSTERIOUS WAYS

Barbara Barrow scored birdies on five of the last nine holes to capture her first LPGA tournament, the Birmingham Golf Classic in 1980.

At a post-tournament gathering, Barrow told friends and fellow golfers, "I want to thank God for my short-game success." It's not unusual for athletes to credit a Supreme Being for their achievements, but Barrow spelled out exactly why she was crediting God.

She said, "God knew I couldn't putt, so He put me closer to the hole."

AT LEAST THEY WEREN'T GUTTIES

Visionary television golf pioneer Fred Raphael had never picked up a golf club until he was tapped to produce *Shell's Wonderful World of Golf* in the early 1960s. Only then did he take up the game.

One time, Raphael, who was still very much a duffer, played Pine Valley Golf Club using some balls that he had been given when he was in London. The next day, the club president called a Pine Valley member who had played with Raphael. The official complained that twenty-eight nonregulation British balls had been found scattered around the course. The member then called Raphael at home to ask what he should say to the club president.

"Tell him to keep looking," Raphael replied. "There are four more still out there."

A WIN–WIN SITUATION

Larry David, creator and star of *Curb Your Enthusiasm* and co-creator of *Seinfeld,* admits having a love–hate relationship with golf. He explains:

"I'm happy before I play because I think, perhaps, there's a chance that I will do well. Then when I'm playing, I'm utterly depressed. But when I'm finished playing, I'm thrilled. I'm actually in a better mood, because I'm done with my pain and suffering. It's a win–win situation to be done playing, whether I do well or not."

BAD DREAMS

English golfer Tony Jacklin, winner of the 1969 British Open and 1970 U.S. Open, shared his golf dreams with *Golf Digest* in 2002:

"My golf dreams are appalling. My ball is always in a sink, under a bureau or against a wall where I can't get at it. Or I'm forced to hit my ball through a sliding-glass door that is barely open. Last week I dreamed I was playing through a sea of snakes, with a giant mother python guarding them. Just once I'd like to dream of winning a tournament or something."

The great Byron Nelson, who once won eleven consecutive tournaments on the PGA Tour, told the magazine in 2003 that he never dreamed about golf when he was an active player between 1935 and 1946.

"The dreams started after I quit," he said. "There was a pattern to them: They started out good and ended bad. I'd be at a tournament and leading, and I couldn't find my shoes. Or I couldn't find the entrance to the clubhouse. Or they'd be calling me to the first tee and I couldn't find my way there. If the dream got as far as me actually teeing off, I'd need a certain club and it would be missing. I don't care who you ask, golf dreams are rarely good."

FIREWATER

Flamboyant golfer Doug Sanders never forgot his roots while he was on his way to winning twenty PGA Tour events and golfing with Hollywood stars.

He still made the same kind of moonshine that his poverty-stricken family brewed back in Cedartown, Georgia, during his childhood in the 1930s and 1940s. The hooch, which was about 190-proof, wasn't clear like grain alcohol but more like the color of Coca-Cola.

During his playing days, Sanders always kept a gallon or two of white lightning at his home to share with guests after a day of golfing with them. Most of his guests had never tasted such homemade booze and were eager to try it, especially golfing buddy and "Rat Pack" entertainer Dean Martin, who was never known to turn down a drink.

Sanders gave Martin a small glass with the standard warning. "This is not like whiskey," the golfer said. "Take tiny sips, or you'll be in for it."

Martin didn't believe him. The entertainer took a big swig and swallowed it. He had just poured the rest of the moonshine into his mouth when his eyes grew wide and his knees grew weak. Just then, Sanders began to light a cigarette. Martin sprayed the hooch from his mouth onto the floor and shouted, "Don't light that smoke! You'll blow my head off!"

FROM BEYOND THE GRAVE

Australian pro and trick shot artist Joe Kirkwood played in exhibitions all over the world and won several PGA Tour events. He also was a noted golf instructor and even gave some lessons to the Queen of England.

NASTY SLICE

Shortly after winning an Academy Award for best supporting actor for his role as a crusty old priest in the 1944 classic film *Going My Way,* Barry Fitzgerald, an avid golfer, accidentally decapitated his Oscar while he was practicing his golf swing in his house. Because it was wartime, the coveted statuette was made of plaster and broke easily. His studio, Paramount, paid $10 to replace it.

Ironically, Fitzgerald had earned the Oscar for portraying a priest who hated golf, Father Fitzgibbon. In the film, Father Chuck O'Malley (played by Bing Crosby) asks Father Fitzgibbon to join him for a round of golf. Father Fitzgibbon declines, asserting, "A golf course is nothing but a poolroom moved outdoors."

At the age of sixty-six, Kirkwood became the Stowe (Vermont) Country Club's first head golf pro after the course was expanded to eighteen holes in 1963. He died seven years later, but not without leaving the golf world with a little mirth.   ·

His granite boulder tombstone in a Stowe cemetery bears this epitaph:

> Tell your story of hard luck shots,
> Of each shot straight and true.
> But when you are done,
> Remember, son,
> That nobody cares but you.

ABOUT the AUTHORS

Allan Zullo has penned more than ninety non-fiction books on a variety of subjects. Of the more than two dozen books that he has written about sports, ten are about golf, including *Amazing But True Golf Facts* and *Astonishing But True Golf Facts.* He was the coauthor of the best-selling eleven-book *Sports Hall of Shame* series, which celebrated the wacky and bizarre side of athletics. Zullo, who talks a much better game of golf than he plays, lives with his wife, Kathryn, near Asheville, North Carolina. For more information about Allan, please go to www.allanzullo.com.

Chris Rodell writes about golf and life's other complications from his Latrobe, Pennsylvania, home. He writes for numerous national publications and does all the content for www.arnoldpalmer.com.